Looking Through the Eyes of an Unseen Child

helping them to break the cycle

by Diana Joy

Jennifer Hettman, Illustrator

Proudly Published in the USA by
Books To Believe In, Inc.
(in cooperation with Power Imaging, Inc. of Centennial, CO)
17011 Lincoln Ave. #408
Parker, CO 80134

Phone: 303.794.8888
Fax: 720.863.2013

http://UnseenChild.com
http://BooksToBelieveIn.com

ISBN: 0-9824705-0-9
Library of Congress Catalog Number: 2009930178

Illustrations by Jennifer Hettman

Cover Design by Capri Brock

Back cover photo by Neil McKenzie Photography
www.NeilMcKenziePhotography.com

Julia,

keep fighting

the fight dear

friend! Praise

God for dis'piero"

Joy! Joy

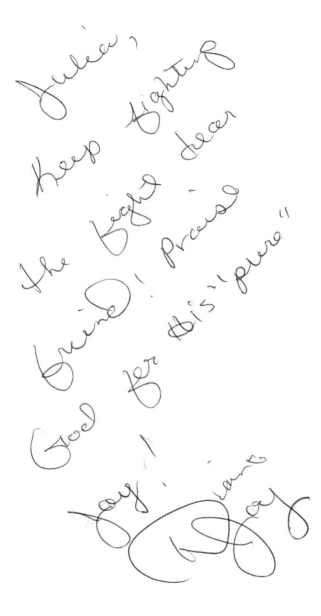

Disclaimer

Due to the author's desire to protect those who are innocent, certain names, dates, locations, and other details have been purposely omitted or changed.

The author(s) reserve the right to speak only of those incidents that are recounted within these pages and to refuse any requests for additional information that are deemed inappropriate or unnecessary.

Diana Joy is sharing her life experiences from her personal point of view only and is not comfortable expressing her unique perspective as the truth perceived by all involved.

For those others who may have been present during these events, you have the freedom to tell your story only if, or as, you choose. She encourages you to do so.

"To know Diana Joy is to now a pure faith and a hope that defies human understanding. Being a part of her life is a privilege; walking beside her has increased my faith and belief in the resiliency of the human soul. It is moving to read Diana Joy's story and to know that others will be touched by reading it too."

Cindy Smith, LCSW

"*Looking through the Eyes of an Unseen Child* is an extremely powerful book, helping to liberate the coversation and understanding of Multiple Personalities Disorder (MPD), but more importantly, to remind us that there are thousands of Unseen Children walking amongst us who deserve acknowledgement."

Michelle Fraas, MSW

"Diana Joy is a hero. She is a woman of enormous personal courage who found the strength to face her disastrous childhood and pull from it the very best lessons of living; love, compassion and forgiveness. This is a tough story to tell and a tough story to read. Based on her own truths, Diana Joy continues to teach us all and, like so many heroes, I am grateful for this lesson."

Dr. Leslie A. Stanwix, D.O.

"Diana Joy takes the reader on an emotional journey through the life of and unseen child. What a gift!"

Sandi Nieves, BA. PSYCH

DEDICATION

I dedicate this book to a special man who had a mission. This is a man who looked at a small, nappy-haired, angry child and felt her pain. Thank you, Gale, for loving me through wonderful moments and painful moments. I appreciate that you honored my fears and never gave me any reason to question the trust I have in you. Though I didn't believe I deserved it, I saw your unconditional love for me in your eyes. When you would smile, somehow I felt pure and special and you gave me hope for my future.

Even as the years came and went, and your attempts to rescue me from the abuse were unsuccessful, I never lost my longing to see the acceptance in your eyes whenever we met. You were and will always be a reminder of the true picture of Christ. You judge no one and welcome all into your house.

Twenty-five years later, when I faced death at the age of thirty-eight, I ran to you and asked for comfort. As I struggled to walk up the sidewalk of the familiar blue house, once again you were there. I felt hopeless as I dropped my cane and you wrapped your arms around me. You said, with tears in your eyes, "Diana, if you go before I do, then wait for me at the gate of

Heaven. If I go before you, I will be there to welcome you with open arms. All the pain will be forgotten and we will rejoice!"

Now that you are aging and suffering with Alzheimer's, I want you to know that your unconditional acceptance is the gift you have passed down to me. With honor, I will embrace all the lessons I learned by observing you. I pray I can walk in the footsteps you walked. Your mission to see the unseen children in the world, through this one unseen child, will continue!

BOOK ONE
Diana's Story

BOOK TWO
the unseen children of today...

ACKNOWLEDGEMENTS

I want you, my family, to know how deeply I appreciate the sacrifices you have been asked to make. From the oldest to the youngest, you gave me my reason to continue and you never let me quit, even when I said I was done and couldn't type another word or shed one more tear.

Dave, my dear husband of more than 20 years, all my love and respect to you for the many times you played both dad and mom to the children while I struggled through my past.

There are so many special friends and church families that have been a part of my life, that there are not enough pages to list them all. And I couldn't just list a name without wanting to share the whole story of how you each supported me and brought me to where I am today. So, it is from the bottom of my heart that I thank you all for your unending love.

And to those on my book writing team – who was the one who said this would only take six months?!? Five years later, we're still typing the last paragraph...

Jenny, I'm so sorry for the constant phone calls begging for just one more picture and promising every time that it was the last one.

Diane, thank you for keeping my office, and my life, organized during this project.

Paula, Denise, and all the others who have volunteered their time and talents at various stages in this work, I thank you.

Additionally, I want to acknowledge all those who have supported my health needs. These include the many doctors, nurses, therapists, mental health workers, counselors, teachers, case workers, ambulance drivers, and all those who have shared their skills to help me survive. Even when you believed it might be best for my health to stop writing, you continued to stand by my side.

And, finally, I, Diana Joy, want to thank all that live within the body. In writing this book, it has seemed like we were being punished for each secret we typed. It was as if the body continued to betray us with illness and pain hoping we'd keep quiet. The fear of even more abuse was so great, that we experienced seizures or heart attacks in order to keep us from sharing the most dangerous truth of all, which is that *we are many that share one body*. This left our healthcare providers in confusion and panic, unable to define the cause of our failing health. But I knew deep down that actually, our true survival was to return to our past and experience the pain and cry the tears, in order to live. Thank you for allowing me to put the words on paper so that others can understand the true meaning of Multiple Personalities.

The greatest of all acknowledgments is to You, God. Because of You, we live today!

FOREWORD

In 1997, B.B. "Robbie" Rossman, Ph.D. *(now deceased)*, asked me to write a chapter for the book she and Mindy Rosenberg were editing. This book, ***Multiple Victimization of Children: Conceptual, Development, Research, and Treatment Issues*** *(Hawthorn Press – 1998)* was my first attempt at publishing work about my thirty-year clinical experience of working with the abused. Many drafts later – after facing fears and tears, with Robbie's unending support, I gave birth to the chapter titled **"Intro to the Haunted House of Mirrors: The Treatment of Multi-Traumatized Adolescents."** My clients, especially Diana Joy, inspired this chapter and now I am honored to witness the conception and development of her book, which adds a unique and personal perspective to the literature on child abuse.

The cruelty of child abuse – be it emotional, physical, sexual, or, as in the story you are about to read, multi-victimization – is paradoxical. These children are often repeatedly forced to seek comfort from the very adults who are inflicting their pain and emotional harm.

Some children grow up to molest their own children. Some survive through prostitution and criminal behavior. Many experience life-long depression, anxiety, post-traumatic-stress-disorder, eating disorders, substance abuse, and other mental health inflictions. Those who are fortunate enough to find a caring environment, and those who are courageous enough to learn to trust, can find healing.

Diana Joy's story is not about abuse, but the healing path she chose. Guided by a strong belief in God and the support of her husband, friends, and professionals, she has found the inner strength to live a meaningful and full life. She has the gift of accepting and loving all who enter her life, without judgment. When you read this book, read with eyes of gratitude, not horror or pity. Diana Joy challenges you to join her journey in offering a safe, trusting place for the abused children and adults of the world.

Dr. Donna B. Marold, Ph.D.
Licensed Psychologist / Licensed Marriage and
Family Therapist
Adjunct Faculty – Regis University

Karen, Diana, John Junior, Denise, Timmy and Sam

BOOK ONE

Diana's Story

Chapter 1

Letter from Diana Joy

My story was so painful and I felt so ashamed that it was hard to tell. I knew that I must write about the secret journals that I kept hidden from all, though the journals were originally written only for God. He was the one that heard my cries. Please read these painful words without judgment. In writing this book, I realized how many parts there are to me. For many years, I felt such shame and separation. Now I know that I don't need to escape from what is... I can embrace my life to find unity and healing.

I'm Diana Joy and I came to be on Sept. 11, 2003 – the day my foster children were removed from my care. I started writing this book to address the accusations made regarding my ability to parent effectively. These accusations were based on the record of my diagnosis with Multiple Personalities Disorder (MPD). The questioning of my ability to parent well proved to be unfounded, and my children were returned safely home again.

My purpose in writing this book was not to traumatize, but to educate society about my understanding of the characteristics of Dissociation.

I'm here because I chose to love – those within and those without. I put the words on paper for those voices only I can hear, and the faces only I see. This book is a gift from God and an open letter, both to those in my personal life, and to all those who find their own truth in my story...

To my oldest daughter,

You will never know how much you helped me come to this point in my life. It is not a birth certificate that made you our daughter, but your big blue eyes and your small smile as you wandered through our apartment building on many late nights, years ago. You were only eight when you were found peeking through our window and knocked at our door. You always asked the same question, "Can I baby-sit?" At first, I giggled at the thought of such a young girl wanting to care for a boy almost her own age. I wish I would have listened to my heart, and looked in your eyes at that time. Why didn't I question how such a small child was allowed to wander through the apartments alone? You never used words to explain how much you were hurting. Then a few years later, when you were eleven, you finally found the courage to tell us of the abuse you were suffering. But, because I had not yet accepted my own past, I denied the truth that you attempted to share with me. It was my own fear that pushed you to become a runner and live with a shame that wasn't yours.

My dear daughter, it was the phone call you made at thirteen, from the institution for difficult juveniles that changed my life. When I saw you, again, your pain mirrored my own, and guilt consumed me for having failed you, just as others failed me. I decided then that I would use adoption and foster care as my

way of helping you and other children to be 'seen.'
Still, it wasn't until you had children of your own,
that I saw your trust in me return to your eyes. You
are still my silent child who chooses not to speak of
your shame, and so I will now speak for you... It is
not your secrets I will reveal, but mine. Thank you for
teaching me the greatest lesson of all – because you
forgave me, I can find forgiveness for others.

To my twin sister,

I want you to know that I remember the day we
said goodbye some 30 years ago. It was a cold
Thanksgiving Day that we realized we were no longer
able to stay together. We were wet up to our knees on
that windy day as we shared our meal on the
sidewalk curb. The many people who drove by just
splashed us with wet snow, as though we were not
even there. We shared a piece of pizza and a can of
soda, purchased at the only store across the main
road through our small town. "It's time to say
goodbye, I'm cold, and I'm tired," you said, with your
tearless eyes. We clung to each other, our small, frail
bodies carrying the worries of an adult. We knew the
only way to deal with the guilt was to run and escape.
It was beginning on this day that we walked very
different roads in life, living with anyone who would
take us, though never finding a place to call home.
Any attempt to contact each other only revealed our
deep, bloodstained scars. It was many more years
later, the need to feel complete drove us together
again. Thank you for your recent phone call and your
willingness to open that painful door we closed so long
ago. I heard your rage when you sobbed "Tell the
story, Diana, I want them to know what they did to
us!" It took my breath away when you whispered, "I

want you to know I tried to stop them." The words were too much and too painful to continue, and soon a dial tone is all we shared.

To my siblings,

I'm ready to tell the story of how the six of us did not ask for the life we were given. I will open my journals and share many memories of our childhood. My memories of six small children lost along a horrendous road, trying to rescue each other from abuse, only to find the fight too hard and the road endless. I want you to know I still grieve today for the many years we lost. We were unaccepted by society, burdened by the unspeakable abuse. This drove us to go distinctly different ways in life, each of us believing our chosen path was the answer to our own survival. My hope is in the telling our secrets, you will find the courage to heal. I tell this in defense of us all.

To society,

I'm writing this book for you – the parents, teachers, counselors, doctors, and all those who have children in their care. As a mother, I know that sometimes, no matter how hard you try, some things fall apart anyway. I hope that by revealing my life experiences, I save a child from suicide, an act of murder, or becoming part of a gang. As I share my journey with you, realize that many children feel unseen and are at times, forced into the dark shadows of life. Please, take responsibility and stop hiding from the truth! Don't become another stranger on the street...

To the Unseen Children of all ages,

You know who you are. I know this is painful, and for that I am sorry. I want you to know you are not alone and mine is not the only story you will find in these pages. You will find opportunities to look through the eyes of some of the many children who have become a part of the family my husband and I have created. You will read about their past, as well as the reality of the world they live in every day. I have held many young hands and cried through too many funerals. It is because of their words, pictures and the bravery of these young children that I have the dedication to tell what is true. I understand that your fears may tempt you to put down this book and keep running. But don't! We need you! Stay with us through our heart-wrenching memories. My prayer is that, no matter what your challenges, you will find the strength to walk with us and discover hope, healing, and faith.

After many years of therapy, my view is that an important part of my survival was not only to accept my multiple personalities, but also to shed many tears for the loss of a family that could have been. The journals I held may not be the same as my siblings. We all look at life differently...and our past has different meanings. *So, embrace your memories and realize that each road we took made us who we are today.*

Chapter 2

The Chair

It was 3:00am, the morning of September 11, 2003. The flashing lights from my clock lit the room. It was too early to be awake... a heavy sick feeling rested in my stomach... Was it the memory of my husband's family, and the friends they lost this day, two years ago...? Or could it be that this day held something even more frightening...? My mind drifted back...

My husband was born and raised in New York before he traveled out west to attend the Bible College where we met, in the early 1980's. We were married shortly thereafter. The mid-west became our home, and New York City was where my new in-laws lived. After twenty years, I felt like I was part of this large family and New York was my favorite place to visit, with so much love and happy memories. Every visit meant an incredible view of the Twin Towers from my in-law's window. The same view shared by so many people on their way to work everyday, each with a different face, and a different story to tell. The morning of the attack seemed like any other morning. I was in my home switching the channels on the television when, in a flash, fear filled the air. A plane had hit one of the towers, and within minutes, another plane went soaring through its twin. Instantly, a blanket of confusion and grief covered the United States.

Knowing that my brother-in-law worked as a New York City police officer, the reality that his life could be in danger caused my family to panic. He managed a brief phone call to assure us that he was alive, but as the phone went dead seconds later, I felt myself slipping. I was losing all my happy memories and the only past I had chosen to tell my children. As the day went by, it felt like weeks. Once again, death was only moments away from those I loved.

The day that America lost so many lives reminded me of my loss also, the loss of my own childhood and the reality of the dark cavity that rested within me. I was no longer able to forget my childhood and to tell only the stories of my life in New York City. Now, this incredible city would be another tragedy from which I must run.

As I layed in bed, I closed my eyes tightly and curled up, wanting to forget about the huge dark cloud and the belief that there was nowhere to hide from danger. It became impossible to escape from the flashbacks of my past. I slowly pulled the covers up over my head and tried to return to sleep. Soon enough, the alarm clock went off and my day began like every other, filled with anger and wrapped in shame. My secrets kept pushing me into a world only I know, and caused me to feel like a shadow forced to wear a mask.

I dragged myself out of bed, the darkness was ever-present around me. Which mask should I wear today? Mother? Wife? Or one of the many other masks I have stored away? I turned on the light and stepped onto the stage we all call 'life.' My anger surrounded me and gave me the energy to walk through the house and wake everybody. As the lights came on, the darkness faded behind my mask. I stumbled down the hall, desperate to make a difference in the lives of my children and the four foster girls currently in my care. As I went from room to room, I prayed the rage was not so powerful that the fight to get the children to school was impossible.

My heart hurt at the thought that one of these children might choose to keep their anger inside, if only for the purpose of fighting, hurting, and defending themselves. A child who is unseen long enough will be seen. I only prayed that the child in the next room was seen through a pure wonderful strength and not a rage that can, and has, killed. "Oh, Lord," I prayed to myself, "not this one! Please, let her lift up the blankets and let me see her beautiful eyes, and help guide her to a safe road. Please Lord; don't let it be too late! We have already lost so many, because they were unseen too long. Hear my words, Lord, and give this child a chance." A sigh of relief came over me when I approached the room and the child lifted her body and climbed out of bed. "Maybe this one will trust me, Lord," I whispered to myself. And so, another day began...

My hope is that you can understand life as it is seen through the eyes of an unseen child. It is only a glance into a child's eyes that can change their world. This is why I need to share the pain from deep inside of me, so that you can see those young eyes, before the feeling is too old to erase, and the mask is painted to perfection, and the ability to be seen is so difficult, that only the anger can make one move to hurt or to help another child hidden in the shadows of life.

The day continued to be a day filled with many emotions hidden behind my mask. "Why does my body continue to hurt today?" I wondered. I heard a young voice inside of me warning that danger was near. The darkness was no longer a sick feeling in my stomach; it was taking over.

As I arrived home from school with the children that day, there were two caseworkers standing in the driveway. The children and I looked at each other and knew something bad was about to happen. There was no time to discuss these intense feelings. We were surprised by this turn of events.

Once we were all in the house, the two caseworkers announced that they were there to take two of the foster children. They offered little explanation. A tall older male caseworker entered my front door and announced, "I have one of the four children with me." The look in this caseworker's eyes caused a feeling of panic. Soon many people came in, without knocking and, without looking into my eyes.

My heart pounded out of my chest! "What is happening here?!?" I yelled. I screamed for my husband. The room began to spin as if I was on an amusement park ride. It got darker and I struggled to look into someone's, anyone's eyes. It was as if I was a child again. "What did I do wrong?!?" I screamed. My voice echoed throughout my dark shadowed body. The mask was coming off. "They are taking my babies away!" I screamed. "Look at me, someone, please!" I walked around the house as if I was five years old again and could not find my way. I bumped into walls while walking down the narrow hall towards my children's room. When I saw the one tall male caseworker again, he didn't look away. I saw the tears in his eyes. He held me close, "It will be alright," he assured me, but his eyes did not.

The foster children screamed, my own children screamed. I stayed next to the tall caseworker and I heard him quietly say, "This is the worst day of my life!" I looked up and he would not look at me anymore. He walked away.

I was left as a shadow in the hall. A whirlwind of activity surrounded me, mattresses lifted and moved, dressers torn apart as clothes were stuffed into plastic bags. The only sound I could hear was my husband's cry, "My children will not leave our house with their clothes in plastic bags!" He opened the closet and grabbed suitcases.

All I could do was look at my feet. I knew the people in my house were not looking at me. I was ashamed; my mask was off. I cried, "Why are they taking my children away?" But I knew why they were taking them. It was because of me. It must be the dark me that caused all bad things to happen. It was only in the dark, or in the shadows that eyes quickly turn away. I sat at the desk in the kitchen away from the screaming, away from the way of the caseworkers and children, and attempted to hide.

A small voice cried, "I'm afraid, mommy!" I realized that I was not the only one hiding; my six-year-old daughter was hiding in a corner under the desk. I wanted so much to climb under the desk with her. I sat on the floor, and held her close, "It will be alright honey."

My husband approached me and reached his arms out to hold my child tightly. The whisper of her voice faded as I followed the last two girls out the door and they headed towards a car. The thirteen year old, (who I knew had been in 25 homes since she was six) looked into my eyes as I held her in my arms. She screamed as the caseworkers pulled her away from me, "Mommy, please don't let them take me away!" I held on to her as long as I could, then the pain was too intense. Her tears fell onto my face. I let go. I will never be able to erase the image of these two girls, with their faces pressed to the back window of the car, crying as they drove away.

Everything seemed to go black and I vomited as I fell to the ground. A voice inside told me, "You need to get up and go back into the house." As I stumbled toward the house, I heard the sound of my husband crying. He was in the living room on his knees wailing. I numbly went to hold him. As I held him, my six-year-old daughter said, "Mommy, please do not let them take me away!" Those words echoed through my trembling body. I realized I had never cried out those words. The reality of that realization shot a piercing feeling of rage and pain throughout my body. At that moment, time no longer existed. It was no longer September of 2003. I stepped backwards in time, backwards into a world that I had fought so hard to forget. I was a small child sitting in a large chair, no longer a mother, or a wife.

I flashed back to a dark and empty room. A tall blond man with dark blue eyes glared at me. His eyes were so dark that I knew I was about to face an unbelievable punishment; a consequence that was dangerously unknown. I sat in the chair. I tried so hard to sit up straight, (as to not make those eyes turn into fire). But the voice boomed and my body trembled.

Peter & Diana

"NO!" a voice quietly whispered in my ear, "You must not make the creature angry." I knew this voice; it was my friend, Peter. He was always there with calming words of wisdom warning me of the possibility of danger. He has kind, dark blue eyes and was somewhat bigger and definitely stronger than I was. He stood next to me to remind me of the rules of the night as I sat in that painfully big chair. "Do not move... do not speak... just listen."

I wanted to go to bed and lay down safely beside my twin sister and close my burning eyes. The smoke-filled room caused me to cough, but I knew it was time to be quiet. He was about to tell me the old familiar story that I hated to hear, the one of my unexpected birth. "You were not supposed to be here," my father began. I knew this story too well and those words filled my heart with anger. He told me that story so many times. I knew it was coming especially after a long day of seeing him with a liquor bottle in his hand. However, I could not show my unspoken rage, as he continued to tell the story. As I did so many times, I looked to Peter for help to get me through it.

"Your mother and I stopped for some food at the grocery store. I waited for her, with your two brothers, and that girl," my father said in an irritated voice. "That girl isn't even mine. It was a good thing I was there for your mother then. She was pregnant with her first child (that girl) by another man and it was 'I' that saved her." As his words continued, he described a young woman, walking through a grocery store not knowing what to get for the angry man. I pictured the fear in her face and her pregnant body rushing from aisle to aisle. I imagined my irritated father waiting in an old rundown vehicle. I saw the dark haired girl, and the two small boys, attempting to reach their heads over the back of the seat. I imagined my father sitting and smoking, with 'the look' that was always on his face.

I took a deep breath and prepared for the rest of the story. As my father talked of my mother, I noticed a change in his eyes, just a slight change, (as if she were special?). He spoke of her as if she was a useless slave, and yet his eyes told you something different. I was so confused by his words and his expressions. I could see a small smile, but it was only visible to someone who had heard and seen him tell this story many times. My mind started to wander, and then I felt myself slipping off the chair. I reminded myself that I must stay awake... I must listen! Every once in a while my father would ask, "Are you listening to me?" I had to be prepared to answer.

He continued, "She was in the store for just a few minutes and then came running out. I knew that she was ready to give birth to my child." His eyes talked with so much pride, my heart ached as he continued. He brought to mind that I was unexpected and unwanted then looked at the chair as if it was empty.

His words came out so easily; it was like he was talking to himself. The instructions were always the same. My mother was dropped off at the hospital, and had his baby. She was not allowed to say who the father was. I knew that was only to keep the police from finding him. The fear of being caught was always on his mind. She kept to the plan he designed, and did not mess up. He told her the plan over and over as if she was not able to understand his instructions. "Now, remember I am not your husband. When I come to see you, I will be your brother. Do not mess up this plan, Deborah!" There was always a threat that something horrible would happen if you didn't do just as he said.

Once, at that point, I somehow slipped in the question, "Daddy, when were you and Mommy married?"

He always mumbled the same response, "I told you, we were never married!" Then he paused.

I asked him again, "How come Mommy has your last name?"

I was ignored. He continued with his version of the story, "Your mom was shipped off to the delivery room and gave birth soon after. She gave birth to a small baby girl that was so beautiful that she looked like a porcelain doll." His eyes talked with so much pride. "Your mother was sent to the recovery room and she was told that her child was going to be taken away due to some questions for drug use."

At this point of the story, my stomach always felt heavy and the pain from the words that followed never seemed to lessen. I often wondered if I was supposed to be on this earth at all.

At a time when a mother should be rejoicing, it seemed as if someone had played a horrible joke on her. As she lay in bed, she felt as though she was having another baby. She screamed to the nurse for help, but she was ignored. The nurse dismissed her telling her that her baby was already in the nursery and that she was not having another baby. The nurse suggested the medicines were making her ill. But my mother screamed again! The nurse lifted the sheets and saw a tiny, curly-black-haired baby coming out.

"That is impossible," cried the nurse, "this baby must have been hidden under your ribs and therefore unnoticed. You now have two baby girls! This baby is in danger, she is way too small. Take her to emergency care with her twin."

My mother was terrified at the thought of yet another baby. A question ran through my entire being, "Did my mother ever want me?"

I wanted to see the smile on my father's face as he came to this part of the story, but instead his emotions were tied to the fact that his perfect plan to escape from the police was ruined. Again, I had to listen to my father's story. "Now it was going to be more difficult to get your mother and us away from the hospital." He paused for a moment, with such an evil smile on his face, "But I was much smarter than they were!"

His voice rose, my heart started to pound, and suddenly, I felt Peter's hand touch mine. Peter made it better when the words my father spoke drilled the pain deeper inside me. I felt relief when I saw Peter. I felt a smile form on my face, as my father turned his head to reach for another cigarette. "Thanks, Peter," I whispered. I talked with Peter, and my father's voice began to fade. "It doesn't really matter if you were meant to be here or not," Peter said. But the words I wanted to hear him say were, "You were meant to be here!" That question lingers still today...

Peter continued, "Soon as he falls asleep, we can play all night!" Peter's gift to me was to make all the hurtful feelings and questions disappear.

I knew I had to sit still until he finished his story, "I came to the hospital, wearing a trench coat, and fooled the nurse into thinking I was out to rescue the two of you. Meanwhile, when she wasn't looking, I slipped each of you in to each pocket. Your mother was released from the hospital a few hours before, and bang! The plan was done!" He laughed so loud that my ears began to hurt.

At that point, I was no longer in the big chair, but with Peter. We escaped to the top of the room and my father's pleasure of telling such a hurtful story no longer caused me pain. Little did he know that he talked to an empty chair now! Peter and I laughed with joy at the fact that we could see his mouth move, but couldn't hear the words. "What a fool," Peter said. I felt as if I had won a wonderful game of hide and seek! My father couldn't see me, but I could see him.

I have no idea how old I was at this time in my life, the story was told so often and it was always the same. My body still shakes as I reveal my reality, and at the judgment that some may have when they read this book. I must write what I know for all the unseen children. For all who are afraid to face the world with the secrets they carry. These secrets, at one time, may have been their only way to survive. I must believe God will give you only what you can handle. God gave me the gift of protectors and friends who took my place in times of pain. Why did He allow all of this to happen to my siblings and me? Maybe so people can see that what I went through was for a reason. This reality gives me the purpose I now need to keep writing. I must believe that God knows the beginning and the end of my life, and not fulfilling my purpose would leave me lost and alone. There must be a point in life in which we all reveal the memories and face the pain. To not do this could only cause the consequences that perhaps even I and my siblings now live.

I ultimately returned to my chair just in time to hear my father's loud voice reminding me that since the beginning of my life, I was one more reason for all his misery. I believed that I had committed a horrible crime and now I was in big trouble. He shouted with pride, "I threw you all into that old run down station wagon and we headed for the border. I knew those idiots would never find me!" My eyes burned from the clouds of cigarette smoke as I wondered why we must always run. I felt too tired to run anymore, but my father's fear had become my fear too.

"It had been two weeks and we were almost to our freedom, then just after we crossed the border, your mother announced, 'I need to stop at a motel.' I had a friend waiting not more than a day away, he was going to let us stay until the coast was clear and we could return." My father was frantic to reach the destination so he went into a rage when my mother made such a request! "We have stopped so many times since you had those things!" We were just things. We were not children to him, only things. He made us, therefore we were his.

"I pulled over and she unloaded the car and took what she needed. It was only a small amount, so that we still had enough to escape, if we were found." I pictured my mother yelling at my older sister and brother to hurry! Karen was five and Sam was four. I imagined them trying to unload the bags along with their smaller, tired little brother, Timmy. I imagined him rubbing his eyes and stumbling as he was pulled into an old motel at a young age of three. My father fully expected his children to carry the responsibility of each other, and also provide for his every need as well.

I gripped the arms of the chair as he told me again that this was when my mother left us. I wondered if she did it to escape his horrible treatment... or maybe she never wanted children. My body always felt empty as my father came to this part of the story.

He explained, "She put you and your twin in a dresser drawer. Then, she took off as soon as everyone was asleep. I just slipped out to buy some beer and when I returned Sam was screaming, 'Mommy went bye, bye. She took my sissy Karen with her!' I shouted back at him, "I've told you before that girl isn't mine, so don't call her your sister!"

He looked down to the floor for a while. I wondered if he was asleep. If he was, then he wouldn't notice that I wasn't paying attention to his stupid story, and I could go play with Peter again. I hated this part of the story, so the thought of playing with Peter was a relief. But my dad lifted his head, and the look on his face confused me. Was he about to cry, I wondered. The look quickly turned to anger as he shouted, "She looked a lot like you!"

I wanted to run! But I just clung to the sides of the chair and put my head down. I was afraid that he was going to start his horrible torture again.

Just then I heard, "Do not leave now little one, be patient. I am here." The soft voice of my own Little Mother whispered words of comfort to me. Little Mother was the kind of mother any child would wish for. She was the kind of mother who sang as her child struggled with a skinned knee or hurtful words from the playground. Her voice was so soothing that I felt my hands slowly let go of the chair.

I looked up at my father, and the fire I feared so much was there in his eyes!

He yelled, "What kind of mother would leave her children in an old motel with barely any heat, on a cold fall night?" It felt as if I were my mother as he

Denise, Diana and Little Mother

looked at me. Why did she leave me to deal with the frightening creature, whose hands could bring so much pain that one had no choice, but to run or die? Maybe it was to erase the terrible mistake she made? But why was Karen able to escape the anger my mother left behind?

My father's anger was building. I felt the room close in on me as his voice exploded, "You were not supposed to be here, and now I will take you out!" I suddenly began to stand up, and I felt his hands grab my small arms. He lifted me up off the floor and I could feel the blood in my arms beginning to pulse. His dark eyes were so close to mine it was as if I could see the darkest devil looking back at me! I felt sick to my stomach and then vomit began to hurl from my mouth. I heard him scream, and felt my body being thrown through the air. I hit the floor with a crash! The room went black.

One moment, I was sitting in the chair, and the next moment I was lying in a pool of vomit. I began to stand up, but his foot came down on my head. "Lay in it!" he demanded.

"What have I done?" I asked.

"You are your mother's child!" he responded in hatred. His foot lifted up and he sat in the chair. He told me to clean up the mess, and then get to bed.

His story was finally over. I wiped the vomit from the floor with an old washcloth. His angry words pounded in my head, "You look a lot like her!" The anger built up inside me. I believed that she knew he hated me, all because I reminded him of what she did to him.

I needed to be invisible now, to stay safe from his eyes. I was no longer just an unwanted child, but I also needed to be unseen. I cleaned up the mess and headed for a mattress on the floor. I saw my twin sister and curled up next to her. I cried out for Little Mother, "Sing to me, I hurt and I can't sleep." I felt her warm arms around me, and then I held my sister tightly. I slowly fell asleep to the humming of her loving voice. "My special friend," I said to myself, before drifting off into the comfort of her arms, "My own Little Mother."

Chapter 3

The Pink Skirt

Time no longer existed for me. One day just ran into another. After the foster children were removed, I lived six months in the memory of my childhood. I woke up night after night, sick and alone, wondering how I would live another day with these horrible secrets? On top of all my personal struggles, I learned that many of the stories were public information. The phone constantly rang with people asking for confirmation of a truth that I refused to accept. Filled with shame, my house became my prison, where I was forced to look back and relive my young life. I knew in my heart that the answer to our freedom as a family was to be found in the forgotten journals hidden beneath the clothes in my closet. Those words I wrote to God assisted me in defending the rest of my life. With all the journals laid out before me, my hands trembled as I reached for the first hard cover. I fought through the tears to understand the scribbled pages. Each page carried me back...

I was three years old and in a station wagon with my brother Sam, my twin Denise, and off to the edge of the sleeping bag was my brother Timmy. He always had a tendency to stay away from the other children. The rain made a beating sound on the roof. I remembered watching the rain fog the windows and making everything outside look so different. The sleeping bags were covered with mud. I wrapped myself up in Sam's coat and felt the warmth.

Sam was a special brother, one that somehow made me feel safe in a world that seemed so complicated. I was convinced that Sam had a special commitment to me that I naturally assumed was obvious to the rest of my siblings. My insistence of always being the one to cuddle with him, or demand to be the only one to sit on his lap was just an example of my belief that I was the most important child in the family.

Suddenly, we came to a stop and were told to, "Shut up and stay hidden!" My father's voice boomed with emotion. The door slammed and we all looked at each other with curiosity. Of course, we all slowly peeked our heads up to look! I expected it to be the police, and we were all going to jail. Instead, the rain blurred my view of a familiar looking woman with a baby on her hip. My father was yelling at her. I heard the baby crying as my father approached the car.

"Quick!" Sam yelled, which always meant that we were to lie down and be quiet. Then, a blonde, blue-eyed toddler was tossed to the back of the car like he was a bag of groceries, and needed no special care. I was stunned! He was crying so loud it hurt my ears, and tears fell down his face. We all stood looking at him in shock! Finally, Sam picked him up and held him. Even though he acted like a baby, he was almost as big as me! Sam always seemed to make things better, but this boy would not stop crying.

My heart pounded so fast. I felt fear for the child. My father yelled, "Someone shut your brother up!"

"My brother?!?" a voice shouted in my head.

Sam hollered above the baby's screams, "Who?"

My father snapped, "Shut that kid up! It is your brother, now no more questions!"

Sam rocked the boy to sleep. All this new information left me angry and confused. I was mad that this child could take my place. If this was my brother then the woman I saw through the fogged window must have truly been my mother. How could I have missed the memory of my own mother? I would surely remember the woman that I longed for so many cold nights. This feeling of loss caused me to creep closer to Sam's lap, but he pushed me away. I put my head in the corner of a sleeping bag and began to weep. I didn't want this baby anymore!

Soon the rain stopped falling, and the sun began to show through the clouds. The boy raised his head and looked my direction, with a smile. My heart began to feel warm and I wanted to be closer to him. As I moved closer, he began to laugh! We all laughed! Timmy really laughed at him and began to clap his hands. The baby began to clap also.

Timmy was happy that the baby responded and asked my father, "What is his name?"

"Well, I think we'll call him John Junior. He will be named after me!" This made my father smile. We all began to laugh! This was the beginning of a long special relationship between the two brothers, Timmy and John Junior. "This is a good day," I thought to myself.

The new child in the station wagon brought with him a smell that was pretty outrageous. Dad opened the windows, but the stink was still there. The only difference was that now we were also cold as well as queasy from the smell. Finally, my father stopped at a gas station. This is when Sam had to take over the parenting role for yet another child. A child that I was convinced was too big to be in diapers! Sam was also expected to steal food, cigarettes, and anything else we needed to survive. Timmy ultimately was called to step up to the plate and do his part too. Timmy became very good at stealing, and so Sam was forced to tolerate his position as a parent. Both were expected to perform their duties as my father's personal slaves.

I still looked to Sam for safety.

One day, as John Junior, Denise and I played in the backseat, I turned to smile at Sam. He looked back at me and shouted, "What are you smiling about?" Then he turned his head and looked out the window. I pouted and still Sam did not come to my rescue. Shortly after, my father pulled over and asked if anyone wanted to sit up front? My father turned his head around and looked at me. His eyes made my stomach feel strange. This was an unexplainable feeling, so strange that I looked over to Sam to see why this feeling was there. This had never happened before. No child was allowed to sit up front with my dad. He always said, "Children were to be seen and not heard," yet he continued to look at me.

I felt like he somehow wanted me to answer. I said nothing even as the rest of the children screamed out, "I do!" Sam finally glanced in my direction and his eyes carried such sadness. My father said, "Diana, I want you to come up to the front." My brother Timmy shot me an angry look and turned away. I wanted to know why my dad asked me to sit in the front seat of the car. I didn't even say I wanted to. However, I knew I must be obedient to him, so I climbed over the seat and sat down.

I looked at my dirty hands as they lay in my lap. Filled with shame I thought, "Why was I chosen from all the children for the opportunity that was unheard of?" I attempted to distract myself from the uncomfortable feelings within and picked at the strings of my old jeans.

It had been a long time since we had all eaten and, as the car stopped in the parking lot, I was reminded of my hunger. The door opened, and the next thing I noticed was my father's shoes. I began to shake as my father said, "Only Diana can come in with me."

"What! Me! Only me?" I thought. As I lifted my eyes, and looked into my father's face, his eyes looked kind. I quickly ran inside the store, forgetting that we were to never move without his permission. I stopped as I heard the car door close behind me. "Sorry, Daddy," I quickly said, with a quiver in my voice.

"It's okay, sweetie," he responded.

Something was strange, but the food looked so overwhelming that I suddenly forgot my fear. I heard him say, "Pick out one item just for you."

I thought, "Why was I so special to him?" I grabbed a bunch of candy bars off the shelf.

He whispered in my ear, "I said only one." I said, "But, Sam will want me to bring back candy for everyone."

"No! Just one for you," he replied with a stern and quiet whisper. I knew to do only as I was told and so each piece of candy was placed back on the shelf. I had wanted to return to the car, proudly, with a candy bar for each of my siblings, but instead, I held my head down and walked slowly back to the car. Now, I just wanted to take my gift back.

"I'm not hungry," I said. This just felt wrong. It must be a trick, and I expected some horrible punishment awaited me as soon as I was in the car.

As we approached the car, the kids looked at me with anticipation. It made me want to run away! I took the candy bar and hid it behind my back.

I don't know why, but I just climbed back in the front seat. My father announced, "Diana has been a good girl, today!" I could feel my face turn red with embarrassment.

"What did you get?" a quiet voice asked from behind the seat.

I began to hand the candy bar over the seat to anyone who would take it! It gave me relief to give away this confusing gift. Then, as quickly as a small hand grabbed the candy, my father shouted, "Give it back to her!" I did not want it; it was as if it was poison.

Why did he do this to me? I panicked. I didn't want all this attention. Sam always said that we needed to share. My father was mean not to buy something for everyone.

I felt ashamed as he forced me to take a bite. It was not his hands that actually put the candy to my lips, but the unspeakable dark eyes that commanded me to do so. The chocolate tasted awful. My father then grabbed my leg firmly and moved me close to him. I looked back at Sam. I wanted to go to him, to have him hold me, but he continued to look out the window. It was a confirmation of the shame I felt within. I looked down and felt as if I was going to vomit. It was not like Sam to refuse me a reassuring smile. I knew I had committed the unspeakable crime.

"We are almost to our new home," my father announced, "No one will find us now!" I watched the window wipers moving at a fast pace. My father's hand tightly moved up my leg. The tears fell one by one down my cheek, as I pretended to fall asleep. It was just my father and me now. The very moment I had always dreamed of had now become a nightmare. I never want to feel this way again. I cried to myself. Everything went black... I must have fallen asleep...

It was early in the morning when we approached a large brick house. The yard was so green; it even wrapped around the trees and bushes and climbed up the dark walls. It looked like the house was secretly hidden from the outside world. I dreamed of a house similar to the many homes I had seen in pictures, and this looked a lot like it. The car door squeaked open and then slammed shut, which startled me. Suddenly, several thoughts crashed together in my head. I felt a man's hand reaching up my leg. I looked down and was surprised to see only my patched jeans. Then, whose hands did I feel? Did hands even touch me? It couldn't be my father, because he was walking up the sidewalk. I just woke up, so maybe it was only a dream? Yes, it must have been a dream! These questions and more raced through my mind. It couldn't be my father because he never really wanted to hold us or interact with us. Sam was always in charge of our needs.

Fearful thoughts were soon forgotten, as anticipation to explore this new house took over. I began to open the car door. My father quickly looked back at me with that familiar glare in his eyes. It was, again, the unspoken rule, "Don't do anything until I give permission." Without a word, I slowly closed the door, as I watched him stumble up the rocks toward the house. I heard my siblings stirring in the back as I started to wipe the fog from the window, making a small circle with my hand. Now I could see the vines as they intertwined around the windows of the house. I was convinced this house was special!

"Wow! We are in a city!" I never thought it was okay to live around so many people.

My father always managed to keep us away from other children. He always said, "I don't need anyone else; there are too many of you already."

I saw my tall, thin father suddenly stop and begin to struggle with something in his pant's pocket. He reached into each pocket, then looked down to the ground. Unexpectedly, he looked back at me and an overwhelming fear spread throughout my body. Immediately, I found myself in what appeared to be a safe place. "Is this a dream, or is it real?" I thought as I was no longer sitting in the front seat of a cold car. Suddenly I was in a new, mystical world! Filled with wonderment, I walked toward the castle doors that stood in front of me. I was reminded of Sam's enforced rule of 'Finder's keepers, loser's weepers!' Yea! I found this place, so it must be mine!"

My father had found the key and yelled, "Everyone get to work! Empty the car and bring in all of the baggage. Welcome to our new home!" At the sound of my father's voice, my magical castle and the wonderful feeling quickly vanished. My heart pounded as I grabbed a few of my clothes and ran up towards the house; another amazing world yet to be explored. This time my siblings joined me in the new adventure. The five of us now had a safe place that no one could take away.

The door was already open and I looked up at the high ceilings. The floors appeared polished, and the wood glowed. Through one of the windows, I noticed two neighboring children chasing a large yellow bus. We ran through the house and rejoiced at our new discovery. This house would keep us out of the rain and the walls would keep us safe from strangers.

I fell to the floor with laughter and screamed, "I feel free!" I looked around in shock. Surprisingly, no one seemed to care. My father didn't give us the silent look to be quiet or yell at us. We yelled and screamed, and no one outside our house could hear us. Was this what a real family is? My brothers and father brought in a mattress. A small television was placed on an old box in a room next to the front door. This was my father's place of solitude. I heard the sound of my brothers struggling to carry a second mattress to a room at the top of the winding stairs. That is where all of us slept at night, while listening to the television just below us.

The next day, Sam showed us around the neighborhood. I felt a cool breeze as I playfully stomped through the leaves. The little things in life seemed so big to us. We were now free of adults. I played games with my twin sister. Hopscotch was one of our favorites. We learned by watching the kids down the street. We watched other children play games, but always kept our distance. All the while, obeying our father's command, "Nobody comes into the house and don't talk to strangers!"

After a week or two, the feel of the house began to change. The smell of alcohol and cigarette smoke spread throughout the mostly empty house. A cold, dark feeling filled the air. The house that was once our chance for freedom suddenly became a prison. There was never enough food for the five children and we never dared to ask our father for anything. The 'No Talk' rule was always in effect. All it took was a look from my father to confirm whether it was going to be a quiet day, or one filled with endless fear. He spent most of his hours in his room, with the door closed, and I always felt that we were on our own at this point.

The freedom we wanted was not there even when my father was out. On those nights, my father stumbled in late from the bar. We all knew the sound of his mumbling voice as he stumbled up the sidewalk. This was our warning to run upstairs to our room and pretend to be asleep. We all assumed our regular positions – John Junior against the wall, my twin and I would sleep next to each other, and lastly Sam. He insisted on sleeping at the edge of the mattress facing the door. Timmy chose a blanket on the floor. Perhaps he chose this position to avoid being squished between several children. In fact, Timmy was never with the rest of us. Where did he go? How did he escape my father's eyes? How come he got to be invisible? Then, I saw a small red glow from my father's cigarette in the doorway of our room. It seemed to linger for hours. I always wondered why the eerie light of the cigarette caused me so much fear. It was only after the smell of smoke was gone and the doorway to our room was black that I could fall asleep.

Most every day began with the same old routine. Early in the morning Sam woke us up and followed us down the stairs whispering dad's rule, "Be quiet, eat breakfast, and stay inside!" As usual, we all woke up hungry. Timmy opened a can of spaghetti and placed a little on each of our plates. After breakfast, I wandered into the front room. I discovered battered boxes in a corner. My curiosity took over as I began to open each one. I soon found a beautiful pink skirt and a small white shirt. I eagerly took off my brother's hand-me-downs, and happily slipped into my new clothes. Surprisingly, they fit! I was like one of the girls I saw playing outside. I pranced around the house, expecting one of my brothers to see how much of a lady I had become. No one noticed...

Diana

As the day continued, Sam played a game with Denise while John Junior watched with anticipation.

"I want to play," I demanded.

Sam looked at me and said, "Shut up and wait your turn!" I took a deep breath, my face turned red with jealously, and I looked away from the rest of the children. Soon, Sam mumbled, "Okay, it's your turn. This game is called 'Jacks,'" and he tried to explain the rules.

"I already know this game!" I interrupted him, "You don't need to tell me how to play!" I fumbled with the ball, and attempted to pick up the jacks. With frustration, I threw the pieces up in the air, and then raised my voice, "What a stupid game! I'm three years old! I don't want to do this anymore!" It was as if the pink skirt magically helped me grow up.

I wandered around the room restlessly. My stomach began to ache and I ordered to Sam, "You need to feed me now!"

He shouted in return, "Get it yourself!"

I looked around the cloudy, cold room and called out for Timmy. As always, he could not be found, and therefore, would not come when I commanded. I fell hopelessly to the floor and began to pout.

Then, I saw the reflection of a beautiful ballerina in the window, her hair was perfect, her cheeks were red and she stood on her tiptoes. She smiled and whispered only to me, "Hi, it's me, Crystal."

I saw a tattered notebook and a half- broken crayon on the dusty floor. I opened the cover, and on the lined pages, I began to draw a picture of my friend Crystal. She wore a beautiful pink skirt and her hair was pulled nicely up in a bun. I wished that I had her hair, then my nickname wouldn't be "Mop Top." My siblings gave me that name due to the fact that my hair was cut so short and was never brushed. My curls were so entangled that my hair did resemble a mop. That hurtful name was soon forgotten as I stood up and twirled around and watched my skirt flying.

As I came to a stop, I was reminded of my hunger. I glanced around the room at my brothers and sister. I turned my head to the muffled sound of my father's television. With each step I took toward his room, the sound of my sibling's voices began to fade. I stood still with my ear to the door. As the pain in my stomach increased, I knocked lightly. There was no answer. I opened the door slowly and I saw a large, thin shadow lying on the bed.

Instantly, words stuttered out of my mouth, "Daddy, I'm hungry? Can you get me something to eat?" My lips moved, but it seemed as if the voice was that of a different child.

I felt someone take my hand and, as I looked up, I saw a dark-eyed girl. She held her finger to her lips and whispered, "Shh, my name is Diane, let me do the talking."

I started to shake when my father's hands motioned me forward. "Diana, come in, I will make it better," he called. I felt numb as I stepped into the room and thought, "I'm not Diana, I'm Diane." I questioned the smile on my father's face, as he leaned over to switch the channel on the television. It was the sound of my favorite show "Sesame Street" and the voice of "Cookie Monster" that lured me forward.

I looked into my father's eyes and wondered, "Was he happy to see me?"

I ignored the feeling of fear as he lifted me up and laid me down on the bed beside him. I felt the soft sheets and the comfort of the warm blanket. I attempted to pull the blanket up to my face as I started to cough. My father abruptly threw the blanket off the bed. I hesitated with a whisper,

"Daddy, there's too much smoke in here. I want to leave."

I felt such terror as my father's smile turned to anger and he said, "Here is what you need!" He slowly lifted my skirt and a burning pain spread throughout my body. This throbbing feeling was unlike anything I had ever felt before. His hands began to move up and down my legs. I wanted to say, "Why are you smiling, Daddy? Don't you know this hurts?"

I looked down in horror and saw my pink skirt was red. My mouth opened to scream but no sound came out. It was like a nightmare where a monster is chasing you and you scream, but no one hears you. My head began to spin. "My pink skirt is ruined!" I silently cried.

Then I cautiously looked up, and my father's face had disappeared! Instead, I saw my special castle surrounded by fog! The pain was gone and I walked toward my safe place. A girl in the distance called to me. She had a unique voice that somehow made the shame disappear. Through the mist, her face became clear. I was shocked! It was Crystal! She looked like a porcelain doll as she gracefully began to dance. Suddenly, I smiled as I twirled in my beautiful pink skirt!

Chapter 4

Heroes

There was a loud bang!

My castle was gone! I was back on a strange bed, hiding under cold sheets. I held my breath as I trembled with fear. I was confused. Was I in my father's bed? Was I in trouble? The sound of the television confirmed that I was in my father's room. "I can't look," I stuttered.

Suddenly my father demanded, "Get out, Sam!" I peeked over the sheet and found Sam standing in the doorway. Was he searching for me? Or was he still mad at me?

Sam shouted, "Leave my little sister alone!"

Then, there were scary noises surrounding the bed. Even the walls seemed to shout with horrible rage! Unexpectedly, my father turned to me. At that moment, his dark, evil eyes penetrated my soul. I knew it was the end of us! My brother and I would surely die!

Sam kept repeating, "Leave my little sister alone!" Sam's powerful words that followed were those only adults were allowed to speak when angry. Why would Sam use those words? Was he grown up now?

I watched as Sam violently hit my father with a bat. There was a loud crashing sound as Sam threw the bat at my father. I closed my eyes tightly to escape from the painful screams that followed!

A voice within me cautioned, "Do not speak, and do not confront the dangerous man!"

I ignored the warning and yelled, "Run, Sam! I'm okay!"

But, it was too late! Sam could not escape the tall man's anger. I witnessed my brother defending himself from my father's hard blows to his small body. My brother looked like a different child. His body was mangled from my fathers' strong fists and tears streaked down his dirty face. As I saw his pain, I also felt the tears falling down my face. It was as if my entire body was covered in tears. The same terrible, dark red color that stained my pink skirt streamed down these bedroom walls.

Terrified, I attempted to reach for my brother. I started to climb out of the bed, but my legs betrayed me! I fell hard to the floor. I cried out to Sam, "Help me! I'm scared!"

He reached for me and pulled me close. As Sam shielded me from our father, I glanced into his face. In a matter of minutes, my eight-year-old brother's eyes had changed to that of a courageous young man. I felt his hand help me up in such an affectionate way. My legs were beginning to be able to move as he screamed, "Run!" He pushed me out into the hall and slammed the bedroom door closed.

My father's angry voice and my brother's screams faded behind me as I inched my way to the stairs. I moved to the first step and, as I looked up, a sigh of relief came over me. It was Denise! She stood wide-eyed, staring at the trail of smudged red handprints on the walls. I collapsed into her arms and clung to her with each difficult step. She wept endlessly and began kissing me on the cheek. "Everything's going to be okay, Diana," she sobbed.

As we approached the top of the stairs, I saw a shadow curled up in the corner of the hall. I struggled to focus my tear-filled eyes, and I gasped, "Johnny!" I realized that I had just broken another rule, my father's rule of always watching out for the younger siblings... And, filled with shame, I mumbled, "I forgot to take care of my little brother."

I glanced into John Junior's pale face. He showed no emotion and gazed back at us with a blank stare. Denise and I were invisible to him. My twin pulled him close to us, and said, "Johnny, I'm so sorry!"

We couldn't face each other. I put my head down, and could hardly whisper a word, but I knew I must. "Denise, it's my fault... It's all my fault!"

The feeling in our house grew darker than ever before and the air felt unlike anything I can remember. It was as if someone had died... The silence continued through the dark hours as the three of us clung to each other. The night slowly crept by as Sam's words repeated in my mind, "Leave my little sister alone!" Slowly, everything went black... I must have fallen asleep.

Maybe the heavy dark feeling is actually the guilt that I have carried in the depths of my heart. My mind cannot erase the look my brothers and sister had in their eyes that day. Sitting on the top of those stairs, I had no idea that I would someday see so many children, having the same look in their eyes. I realize now that I had to experience that horrible time in my life in order to see a child who is unseen by others.

John Junior, Denise & Diana

(Denise, I hope you know you had the warm arms of an angel on that day. Only an angel could love someone that deeply. You and I are truly twins. I believe that your love, at that moment, was a gift given to me by God.)

I felt the warmth of the sun shining through the window above us. The rays from the top of the stairs always meant that the night was finally over and a new day had begun. Denise had fallen asleep with her arms wrapped around me. I glanced over at John Junior and my heart filled with a dark sorrow. I reached over and laid my sister down with her tiny legs hanging over the top of the stairs. I gave her a kiss on her tear-streaked face. Johnny still had that same tearless, blank look on his face. He sat so still. I glanced quickly over at him in shame. He continued to look ahead with empty blue eyes. This was the first time I had seen my baby brother with such a look of isolation - no clapping, no cute smile on his face and no sparkle in his once innocent eyes. Grief filled my body as I kissed my brother. He continued to look like a statue, as I moved down the stairs to see the remains of the house.

My body shook with pain as I moved down the winding hall. With each awkward step, the pain, fear, and sadness slowly disappeared. It was as if I were becoming a stranger in my own body. As I came around the corner, I saw my father's room. The closer I got, the louder the television became. I wanted to back away from the noise, but strangely enough, my legs kept stepping forward.

The door was open and I peeked my head into the room. I heard a muffled sound from behind the mattress in the corner and my curiosity drew me closer. All of a sudden my feet stopped and my heart began to pound! I quickly looked around for an answer to all the panic I felt within. I knew I needed to run, but I couldn't remember what I would be running from. Peter said to me, "Don't you think we should just run?"

I felt someone gently touch my shoulder from behind. It took my breath away. I fell into someone. It was Sam, and we both fell to the floor and cried. "I'm sorry, Sam! I didn't mean to do it!" Even as I spoke the words, I wasn't sure I understood what "it" was. I could only remember that I was the one that had my shirt torn, and was lying in my father's bed. The sick feeling in my stomach told me that I must have caused all of the dreadful pain.

"Where is Dad?" I asked as my body trembled endlessly.

"He's over there," Sam responded. "I called the police, he's hurt pretty bad." Sam explained that he blacked out during the fight and, when he woke up, our father was laying in the corner next to the bed.

Timmy came into the room. He sat and listened to what had happened. I kept trying to listen, but the more I tried, the more confusing the words became. I realized my shirt was torn and my pink skirt was ruined. I felt so ashamed in front of my two brothers. Sam looked into my eyes and it felt as if he could read my mind. Timmy looked at me and stood up as Sam handed me some old clothes from the box Timmy was sitting on. Denise came down with John Junior and we all sat in silence. As we heard the sirens come up the hill, we heard heavy breathing from my father.

I hesitantly looked up. My father glared at me. "What have you done?" He screamed! I didn't know. I just looked down at my frayed torn jeans and my brother's old shirt.

Sam stood up and walked over to me and he held me close. "My Hero," I said to myself. Then I felt Denise and John Junior's warm bodies next to me. Timmy stepped in between my father and us. There were many loud voices moving quickly towards the house. I tried to look at Timmy, but he would not look at me. He kept his eyes firmly on our father. Sam held us close and guided us towards the door. Timmy stood still. My father glared at us. Today was the first day we faced the true monster. That monster was my father. We were the heroes.

As my brothers, sister, and I sat together, the door flung open with a bang. People came in and the look on their faces made me to want to run and hide. It was the police! We were taught to hide and hate the police. Now they were in our house! People dressed in fancy clothes followed closely behind the uniforms. Women had on dresses that hung beautifully down to their knees. I looked at my old clothes and was now angry. The police grabbed my father, and threw him to the hard floor with a heavy thud. They put handcuffs on him and the room began to spin! People were everywhere. I felt I must run...I must hide! I became enraged and yelled, "I want these people out!"

Over and over, my father kept telling the police that it was my brother Sam who started to attack him. My father pointed to the bat, and the large cuts and bruises on his body. I held my brother's hand during this time. I focused on the guns on their hips, and wondered if I was going to jail. I was the one who started all this and therefore I knew I was the one to be punished! I saw flashes of light coming from my father's room. Soon, a police officer approached my brother. My hands shook and I squeezed Sam's hand tighter. The officer looked at him and said, "Son, step over here, I need you to answer some questions."

Denise cried and I screamed, "Don't you take my big brother away!" Sam let go and walked with the tall man. I turned to look for my twin and she was gone!

Denise had already turned the corner and headed up the stairs. I hurried to follow her. As I stepped into the upstairs room, my sister yelled at me, "Get away from me!" I tried to sit on the mattress beside her. My heart hurt as I started to wrap my arm around her shoulder. She attacked me! She screamed, "This is all your fault! They're going to put Sam in jail! Why did you have to do that? You made this happen! You dummy, I hate you! You're not my best friend anymore!"

I wanted to cry as she kicked me in the leg, but instead I screamed, "Stop that!" We tumbled around on the floor with red angry faces.

A woman approached the room and attempted to pry us apart. I sat up, and my sister gave me an expression that needed no words. I was in trouble and I knew it! Her eyes told me that the fight was not over, it would continue when no one was there.

The woman asked, "Would you like to come downstairs, and join the rest of the family?" This woman must be stupid, why would we want to go down there without Sam! Denise and I just sat on the mattress together. It became us against the world. "Get away from me!" I shouted at the woman. My sister began to swing her fists at her. I was about to jump in the fight, when I saw my sister's arm. Denise's body looked as if someone had beaten her again and again. I gasped as our eyes connected and saw a familiar pain. Did my father hurt her, too?

My heart pounded as a policeman entered the room. He and the woman whispered to each other. I heard Peter yell to me, "Run, Diane! Go get Sam!" I darted out of the room and stumbled toward the stairs! I could feel the pain shoot down my legs. I screamed, "Denise, Timmy, help me!" Then, I collapsed and all went black! The next thing I remembered was that I was on the mattress in our bedroom. Denise was next to me and had her clothes off and the woman was taking pictures of her. I laid helplessly while clicking cameras and voices echoed throughout the once empty room. I reached out and held my twin's hand as I whispered, "Sissy, I'm here! It's me, Diana!" She lay beside me like a beautiful doll. I attempted to get her attention and saw her eyes were filled with such sadness. A lump swelled in my throat as my sister continued to stare blankly at the top of the room. The pain in my legs now spread to my heart...

Unexpectedly, a camera clicked and I felt the woman touching my leg! She was trying to take off my clothes! I closed my eyes tightly, clenched my fists, and held my breath.

Then, all of a sudden I felt free! I was finally safe and once again approaching my castle. "No one can hurt me here," I whispered. I skipped up to the front of the castle and quickly threw the doors open! Now I was wearing a new pink gown that flowed all the way down to my beautiful silver slippers. My soft brown curls hung down to my shoulders, "I'm a Princess!" I was startled by the sound of a child's cry. Two fragile girls held each other. The one with short, brown curly hair and tiny freckles on her soft pink face said, "I'm Dee."

The other girl with long blonde waves encompassing her small round cheeks said, "I'm Sue."

I cuddled their petite bodies on my lap. I noticed the pain in their eyes and softly asked, "Why are you so sad?"

Dee answered, "I don't know." I hummed a special song and continued to rock them gently.

After awhile, Sue jumped off my lap and announced, "Dee, it's time to play!" Dee held my hand and pulled me toward a large tree. We all sat down and pulled fruit from the low hanging branches. I felt such joy, as we played together on a seemingly endless day.

All of a sudden, I heard a loud engine and my body was being forced into the back seat of a car. I hurt, and I was being squished in the back seat which just made the pain worse. My head was spinning! In a panic I asked, "Where are we? Where are my girls? Did I leave them alone? I must have forgotten them!"

I then heard Crystal's familiar voice, "It will be okay, Diane." I felt warm hands holding mine.

"Please don't leave me," I whispered. I searched around for Crystal, but she was nowhere to be found.

Sam leaned over and said softly in my ear, "Diana, I will never leave you again." I looked down and saw my brother's fingers wrapped in mine. I wanted to ask him if he could see Crystal, but I could tell that he had too many other things on his mind.

We came to a stop and we all fought to see the large building beside the car. The Social Worker in the front seat told us, "This building is where children go to find a new home."

Sam looked at the four of us, with great concern and announced to the Social Workers, "We don't need a new home. We have ours."

The man driving peered in the rearview mirror and said, "How are you going to take care of four children, Boy? You're just a child yourself!"

Sam slumped down in the seat and muttered, "I just turned eight."

Denise whined, "Sam, I want to go home."

We all got out of the car and Timmy tried to run ahead of us. Sam caught him by the shirt and snapped, "Timmy, we need to stay together!"

He held my hand and we all stayed close as we went into the building. There were so many people and so much noise! Sam continued to pull us close. He kept his eyes on each of us as a small woman guided us down a long hall. She placed us in a small room and walked away. As soon as she left, Timmy searched the desk and was disappointed to find nothing he could take.

Sam hissed, "Shut up, somebody will hear us!"

These walls didn't reach the ceilings. I climbed on a chair to see what was on the other side. I giggled to myself and whispered, "Denise, you can see more children if you step right here!" Just as fast as she pulled herself up, Sam pulled us both down. By the warning in his eyes, we knew not to do that again. We sat silently and, after some time, I wondered if we had been forgotten, again.

Finally, a Social Worker returned and handed us each a small brown bag full of food. Timmy whispered to Johnny, "Maybe this isn't such a bad place after all?"

The woman asked me to go with her. Sam pulled me close and in a somewhat grown up voice demanded, "No! Why do you want to take her?"

The woman responded, "Your sister has some cuts that need to be examined by a Doctor."

Sam looked straight at her and stated, rather rudely, "No! Some lady already did that at our house!"

I then interrupted, "I don't 'member anyone looking at me?" I tried hard to remember where I'd been cut. In desperation, I pointed to a scratch on my finger and said, "Sam, I want to go and get a pretty band-aid now!"

"No!" he snapped.

Disappointed, I grumbled, "Sam is the boss."

The woman appeared just as frustrated as I felt and said, "Then all of you come with me. It's time to go to your new house; we will deal with this problem later."

After climbing back into the car, I pouted, "Sam is no fun, we can't do anything!" I looked down at my shoes and said nothing for the rest of the ride.

We pulled up in front of an old house. Sam got out first and guided us to the front door. As the door opened, I was surprised to find children everywhere, laughing and playing! My excitement grew as Sam guided us to the corner of the large room. The Social Worker talked quietly to the woman in charge of the orphanage.

Sam pulled on my shirt, and said, "Everyone sit!" My two brothers had gathered together some small mattresses and placed them by a large window. We sat under the window in the sunshine and ate the food from our brown bags. It became a safe feeling to have so much going on around us and yet no one acknowledged us. We stayed together on the mattress until we all fell asleep.

A tapping sound woke me up. I sat up, looked around the dark room, and found children sleeping everywhere. As the tapping on the window above us grew louder, I whispered, "Sam, get up! Someone's out there!"

He lifted his head and looked outside, then signaled for us all to get up. Timmy grabbed Johnny and we all climbed silently out the window. I was shocked to see my father, "Run!" he demanded.

Denise and I held hands as we ran toward a small-framed woman. She pushed each of us into the backseat of an old car and she whispered, "Climb in! Stay low!"

My father turned to this stranger as she started the vehicle and said, "Thanks for bailing me out. I owe you one! Now, let's hit the road!"

Sam squeezed us into position and I moaned, "Ouch! Sam be careful, my legs hurt." I frantically reached for Johnny to make sure he was safe. I was sad to discover that a cloud still covered his eyes as he sat motionless.

I looked over at Denise, and she quickly turned away in disgust. In that moment, it was as if a part of me died. I wasn't sure if she wanted to be my best friend anymore. I turned to Timmy, who glared angrily at the back of my father's head.

I whispered, "Sam, where are we going?" He didn't respond, but as I studied his eyes, I sighed to myself, "My Sam is all grown up..."

In a car crowded with so many children, I felt all alone. Everybody seemed so different... I knew I too was different. Tears filled my eyes and I thought, "I must be the one who makes all bad things happen." I slumped down in the seat and pretended to be invisible.

Chapter 5

The Family Business

We were back with my father and it felt as if we could never escape his horrible torture. Anytime we said or did anything he feared would expose his secrets, unpredictable types of punishment waited for us in the darkness. The battle seemed lost. My father won it when he picked us up from the orphanage and squished us into the backseat of an old car.

We lived in an old motel for a long time. Sam was nearly ten years old and was expected to help run what my father called the 'Family Business.' Young women were beaten by large strangers, and then these strangers would slip small green, balled-up pieces of paper to my father.

Timmy wanted more than ever to be a grown up like Sam and my father put both of them in charge of answering the phone. Timmy worked hard to out talk Sam in an attempt to impress my father. The youngest three of us were on our own. Denise, John Junior, and I lived in dark corners of bedrooms or hid in the closets. Sometimes when the sun was almost up and everyone else was asleep, we were able to sneak from room to room to gather up food. To eat or drink meant a lot of following in the shadows of others, hoping to go unnoticed. At five years old, I knew that it was better to steal, than to ask for what I needed. I spent many nights hungry, waiting for the sun to rise.

Soon after the move, my sister and I started school with other kids. It was not my father that insisted we go, but the neighbors who saw us running around in the early mornings. They demanded that my sister and I get an education. I hid my baby brother in a closet, or outside behind the building, until we returned home in the afternoon.

Going to school opened my eyes to the differences between my twin and I. Even as we were introduced, a distinction was clear – she was the 'day' and I was the 'night.' I had no problem speaking with others but she chose to stay quiet. Denise was more sensitive and aware of our need to stay together. She ignored the teacher's demands to "stay in her seat" and ran all the way across the school to my classroom to be near me. She was willing to fight for our reputation; I didn't care what other people thought. It was as if she knew all the things I didn't and the two of us made one whole child.

With each day that passed my desire to learn increased. School became my home. I was fed there and did not have to hide. I ran and played without the fear of being hurt. I got up as early as I could to escape to school. I wrote in library books, on paper, anywhere I could. I wrote in hopes that someone would find my words and rescue me. I wanted to believe that if I could succeed, maybe love was possible. If I could read, then maybe I would appear to be from a normal family. I wanted to be seen. At first, concentration was hard to accomplish and learning didn't come easy to me, so I struggled through each page. If I had to read in class, I panicked. I would distract the class by claiming someone pushed me, or lean on my desk, so it would tip over causing everything to fall to the floor. But at night, I practiced reading to Denise and John Junior with a flashlight and a library book.

As I learned more each day, my hope grew that maybe we could be rescued. "There must be a way to sneak a letter to one of my teachers?" I thought. But, the fear of my father was too great. I realized the words must not be spoken out loud and the letters could never be found by him. If they were discovered, a horrible punishment would be given as soon as I was within his grasp again.

Each day as I walked to school, a new idea of getting someone's attention was on my mind. At first, I started to sneak my words onto the large lined pages or I would draw my feelings inside pictures. I stood in front of anybody with desperation to be seen. Adults just look blankly at my homework, and did not see the cries for help within the scribbles on the wrinkled paper. My frustration and helplessness grew as the grownups always responded with, "What a good job," and then went on to the next child. It was as if I was invisible. It was such a struggle to get someone to look beyond the nappy hair, and small filthy body.

Eventually, I became confused and questioned why there was a sharp, extreme pain flashing through my body as a teacher gave me a hug for accomplishing a new level in learning. I just wanted those eyes to accept me, to love me and take me away from the world my siblings and I lived in.

I wanted a loving mother and father so much. Sometimes, the pain was so great that I thought if I looked for it I would actually see pain seeping through my clothes. As I watched some other mother or father pick up their child, and saw the joy in their eyes, my determination to be accepted only grew stronger. I wanted to be noticed by any adult who had kind eyes.

I sometimes heard the teachers whisper, "This child needs help!"

"Yes!" I would scream inside myself. However, the help I needed was not the help I got. Spending endless hours outside in the hall for my poor behavior was not the help I was crying out for. However, I could not risk using words to explain what was happening. I was only five years old, and I was already losing the belief that words could actually save us...

Nothing made sense in my world. The love I wished for caused so much pain. The longing I felt only caused me to push away from any kindness that was offered. It was only moments after a pat on the back, or a hug from a teacher, and I would go into a rage. Why was I so angry? The only hands that could comfort me were Peter's and Little Mother's and my other friends that only I could see. They were becoming a daily part of my life. I needed them and they needed me. Their touch was so slight and never quite enough, but being with them was my only safe place. I constantly found myself asking, "Is this love?" I started to believe I needed no one else. Even my siblings began to look at me with confusion.

One afternoon, I came running home from school with excitement at the fact that blue and yellow paint mixed together created green. I could take many colors of paint and put them all together to make a picture. Learning was more to me than letters and numbers. I was taught that secrets could be hidden within a picture, and for a moment, some hope returned. My teacher showed us one large painting of kids playing on a playground. Then she asked each student to find a shape or a hidden item throughout

Sue, Dee, Diana & Peter

the drawing of children running and climbing on some bars. I silently screamed, "This was a new way to tell our secrets and be helped!" As soon as the school bell rang, I waited for Denise. I shook with anticipation and longed to see the look in her eyes about my good news.

Denise and I came around the back of the motel, but John Junior was not hiding in his usual spot! I pushed my way through the back door and I suddenly felt two large hands grab my waist. I was afraid to look up, or even down for that matter! I closed my eyes tightly and struggled to break free. I realized that my feet were no longer touching the ground. The smell from the large man caused me to fight with more force. I screamed, but the louder I got, the more I heard laughter. I opened my eyes and my baby brother closed the closet door, and a pile of clothes slowly surrounded him. I knew by the beating of my heart, that I was in trouble! I screamed at the man, "Don't laugh at me!"

A familiar mood was in the air. It told me that 'the game' was about to begin - again. "Shut up child, it's time to play," a deep voice whispered. His words were so close to my ears, that it sent shivers through my body. I turned and saw a stranger's face and was shocked to see that his arms were much larger than my father's. He held me so tight, I was scared I would stop breathing at any moment. The room got darker, as this man put me down on a large bed. Someone else closed the curtains. It was no longer daytime, the terror of the night was upon me.

I kept looking up at the smoke stained ceiling, as I felt soft clothes being thrown on my body. This man must know my father. Suddenly I heard my father say, "Get up Diana, you know how to do this." His voice sounded as if I was now his trophy, for anyone to touch. He sounded insistent and angry. He said, "Remember what I taught you, now show him." I heard my father's voice fade and the door slam!

My hands trembled as I put on the soft satin dress I was just given. A strange familiar feeling overcame me. It felt like I had done this before, but I had no memory of ever having such pretty clothes. So I quickly stood on the large bed to look in the mirror and see how beautiful I had become. As I strained my eyes, I could see a small child that looked like me, and yet her eyes appeared as if they belonged to someone much older. I pulled the dress on to my shoulders in an attempt to make it fit. In the reflection, a large shadow of a man approached me. He then placed something small into my hand. As I held it up to my eyes I could see the bright red color. It was lipstick! Only big girls are allowed to have this. "I must be a big girl now," I proudly announced to myself.

"Put it on," the stranger motioned for me to put the lipstick to my lips.

I again trembled with fear and begged him, "I don't want to play this game anymore! I don't want this gift! Let me go, my Denise and John Junior need me!"

The scary man responded angrily, "Put it on your lips! You belong to me now!" My hands shook as I attempted to rub the lipstick to my lips. I suddenly lost my footing and fell to the floor.

As I attempted to hide from the horrible man, I suddenly saw a person under the bed. Maybe it was my Sam? Maybe he would jump up and rescue me at any moment. As I pulled my head closer to the bed, I saw that the eyes were not Sam's, but those of a kind woman. Her pale white arm reached toward my cold body. She whispered, "Don't worry, he can't see me." I attempted to crawl towards her.

Diana

The large man pulled me onto the bed and demanded, "Get up little lady! Now dance!"

My body began to move as if I was on a stage. By the clapping sound and the light from between the curtains, I knew that the show was about to begin. "Yes, that's it! I'm a Dancer!" I giggled. I held my head up high, lifted my arms and twirled, just as all beautiful dancers twirled. As I continued to balance on the bed the clapping grew louder.

In an instant the scary man grabbed me and pushed me to my knees! His voice felt as frightening as thunder as he yelled, "Come on girl, get under the blankets." I could not breathe as his weight caused me to sink deeper into the bed. I tried to move my lips, to scream for help. Soon, I felt my body hurt, and I felt a slap across my face. I heard a snap, and felt a sharp pain in my jaw. Then all went black.

It was the early morning sun peeking through the drapes that woke me. I attempted to sit up, but I couldn't. The scary man had trapped me with his strong arms. As he rolled over onto my small body, I was convinced I would surely die! All went black, again.

When I woke up next, I wondered, "Am I dead?" A deep sadness surrounded me and I sobbed, "No, I'm still alive. This is what happens when I agree to dance." I looked around the room and cried to myself, "Now I have to stay at the motel. I should have said 'No!' It's all my fault!" As shame filled me again, I mumbled, "I can't break my father's rule now. No one is allowed to see the cuts and marks on me. The motel will be my prison and the school is no longer my safe place to run."

Where were John Junior and Denise? I panicked! I tried to get up, but the more I fought, the weaker I became. Then, in an instant, I was no longer trapped!

I stood beside the bed looking at a small curly-haired girl lying on the bed. I said to myself, "She looks like me, but how can she be me? I'm standing by the bed, I'm not the one on it? I wonder what her name is?" I wanted to hold her and make things all better, but I knew by doing this it could wake the man. It appeared as if the small girl was sleeping, but I questioned if she was only pretending. I thought, "If she was truly awake, she would just say no, and the man wouldn't do bad stuff to her. Yes, that's it, she must be sleeping. When she wakes up, everything will be fine, and we'll play together."

I was startled by a slight touch on my shoulder! My heart was beating so loud that I was sure the whole world could hear it. I closed my eyes tightly. Then I heard a calming voice, "Diane, it's me." I expected to see Crystal or Little Mother. But, I was shocked when I noticed it was the same woman who had earlier reached out to save me from under the bed.

"I'm safe," I sighed.

As I looked into her eyes, I thought I saw a tear. I tried to tell her that all I had wanted to do was dance, but her soft fingers covered my mouth. She pulled me down under the bed and covered me with her robe. I felt so weak and tired. I told her, "This isn't a safe place! That man will look for me here."

I was sure I was in trouble. She quietly said, "My name is Ruby. You've done nothing wrong. You will be safe with me. I've come to take your place. He will not find you, only me." I felt the pain slowly leave my body. Now I knew the little girl on the bed would be safe, too.

Suddenly, someone was pulling me. I found myself back beside the sleeping stranger. "How did I get up here?" I wondered. I looked over and realized the small hands tugging me belonged to John Junior. The man's heavy arms shifted, giving me the freedom to go to my brother and we crawled to the closet. I was comforted to see Denise open the door and motion for us. Then she safely closed the door behind us and held us until she fell asleep. I found myself longing for Ruby's kind eyes and the safety of her arms. She was much stronger than I was. My brave new friend took my place when the pain was too great.

While I sat squished in the back of the closet, I pictured my own beautiful daughter giggling with excitement. I heard myself whispering, "When I'm all grown up, I will keep my kids safe."

I laid my head on my knees and my mind drifted as I said to myself, "Someday, I will be just as brave as Ruby and as wonderful as Little Mother. I will listen to my little girl as she explains to me how blue and yellow makes green. I will tell her how she can see many shapes and fun things hidden in a picture. My daughter and I will play hide and seek on the school playground. I will hold her tight and tell her that she won't have to hide. I will protect her from the big scary people."

After several hours, the door to the motel room opened, and I heard my name being yelled out! "Oh no, my father is here! What game does he want me to play now?" I cried quietly. I knew I couldn't win any game with him.

No matter where I hid, he always found me. Again, he yelled, "Diana, it's time to play hide and seek!" Denise quickly wrapped her arms around John Junior and me and we all ducked our heads to hide.

As my father's voice bellowed, I heard Ruby's voice, "It's okay, my little one. Remember, when the pain gets tough, close your eyes, and I will be there for you."

I thought, "My Ruby is a special friend." I took a deep breath of relief and whispered, "I must be the luckiest girl in the whole wide world to have friends who love me and will keep me safe!"

I climbed even further back into the closet. Denise was there waiting. She wrapped her arms around me. She had a look on her face that told me something bad had just happened. She leaned over and softly said, "It's okay, Diana."

I was very confused and responded, "Why are you telling me it's okay, when I was just with Ruby?" I tried to convince my twin that nothing bad had happened to me, but she just patted me on the back. I felt my face turn red with anger and I pushed her away. "I told you, nothing happened!" I snapped and pouted.

The closet became our own special school and we took blankets and pillows from the beds to make little chairs. The small, unnoticed areas around the motel became our playground. Before I knew it, each day was over and the sun shone through the crack at the bottom of the closet door reminding us that it was time to come out and explore. Even though we were out of the closet, we knew to stay away from the eyes of the people who moved above us. We could not risk being found by the adults in the motel or the neighbors outside.

After many days of sneaking from room to room, one of the girls at the motel found the three of us playing. I never asked her name... All that mattered was that she could keep our hideouts a secret. She smiled as she peeked into the closet or found us playing behind a bed. We laughed and squealed with joy, this game of "hide and seek" was fun. She was our special friend.

One night as I peeked out the closet door, I saw her sobbing. Her body shook as if she were afraid. She was curled up next to a bed and whispered to someone, but I couldn't see anyone there. I climbed out through the heap of clothes and inched my way closer to her. She was holding a small book with a tattered cover. I watched her lower her head and look throughout the pages. I sat next to her, but she didn't look up. It was if I was invisible. She then closed her eyes and I thought maybe something was wrong with her, so I touched her shoulder softly to see if she was awake. She jumped and looked at me in shock, then quickly hid the book behind her back.

I demanded, "What are you hiding?"

She said, "This is a special book about a Person who is stronger than your father. This Man will rescue you."

Her words gave me hope! I felt so special that she was willing to share her unseen friend with me. If she could see Him, then maybe someday I would too. She looked at me with such compassion on that dark night and then handed me the book. Even through her pain, I saw a small light in her eyes. She said, "He will always keep your secrets."

Boy! I was counting on that promise! From that point on, I would ask this Unseen Protector to give me the courage to survive. I made a new book written just for this Special Man named God.

I was almost six years old, and I depended on her daily reassuring smiles. Then one day, as I was anticipating her arrival, she didn't come. Denise said, "Dad yelled at that girl and she told his secrets."

I held the book she gave me close. It seemed like just a day or two and we were on the run, again. We headed for the mountains. If we screamed for help in the mountains, who would hear us? The girl is gone. But, it'll be okay because now I have Ruby, Peter, Little Mother, and now this new, special friend named 'God'.

Chapter 6

The Master

Darkness surrounded us as we sat in an old station wagon and sped up a winding narrow road. My father looked back at me with his dark evil eyes and I knew I was in big trouble! The silence in the air told me that it was just a matter of time until I would be punished. But, what did I do? My mind searched for an answer to the shame I felt deep inside me. I grabbed Denise's hand, but she just pushed me away and moved closer to Sam. I was afraid and felt all alone. I rested my head on the familiar musty sleeping bags and wondered, was it that girl? Did she tell my father about our secrets?

Tears fell down my cheeks as I whispered quietly, "Yes, that's it. She must have been the one who talked to my father. But, she did nothing bad so it must be me who is the bad child. I caused all this to happen!" As I remembered her eyes and her pretty smile, my body ached.

My heart pounded loudly; I sat up and frantically whispered to Denise, "Where is the book that girl gave me? The special book, the one that will tell me how to find God?" In a panic, I searched until I felt the hard cover beneath the clothes. "Finally!" I sighed. I held the book close to my heart, just as I had seen the girl do so many times. "Maybe this book will show me this Unseen Friend of hers? Then maybe God will take me back to her," I whispered as I stuffed the black covered book into my pillow. "I will write letters to this new friend, God, so He will know how to find us! He is bigger than anyone in the whole wide world and He will know what to do."

After several hours of bumpy roads, we came to a stop. My father yelled, "Everyone, get some sleep. Sam, you and Timmy get me when the sun comes up."

I snuggled close to Denise and was surprised to feel her arm wrapped around me. What? She's not mad at me anymore? It wasn't long after I had fallen asleep that my father yelled at Timmy, and Sam, "Come on boys, move it!" My brother's started muttering complaints to themselves.

I attempted to wake up Denise. "We can get up now!" I said with excitement.

She didn't seem as happy and moaned, "Go away!"

I ignored her and climbed over her small body, only to find that John Junior was curled up on the other side. Even though John Junior was nearly five and I was almost six, everyone said he was much bigger than me or my sister. That was something I refused to accept. I always walked in front of him on my toes just to make sure I was taller. I made us stand back-to-back every day. I needed him to know how important it is to be bigger, because whoever is bigger is the boss. I looked up at him and yelled, "Yep, Johnny, I'm still bigger!" He looked down and nodded in agreement.

I decided that it was time to explore and I headed toward the trees. Sam yelled to me, "Diana, don't go too far! You might get lost!" My body froze. It never occurred to me that being lost was something bad. Frustrated, I sat on the back of the car waiting for Denise and John Junior. I decided to wait, and then it wouldn't be so bad if we got lost together.

My father continued instructing my older brothers to put up the tents. I sat watching until my father yelled, "Diana, get out of the way!" Something in the tone of his voice was much different than it was in the motel. Just when I thought things were going to get better, it had become worse. In what seemed like such a small amount of time my father had changed.

"Daddy, can me, and Johnny, and Denise go to the creek?" I asked.

He said, "Sure."

I yelled to my sister and baby brother, "Let's go!"

Then, just as my siblings were finally up and ready to go, he yelled, "No, just Diana! You two stay here!"

"What!" I responded, "I can't go all by myself, 'cause Sam said I could get lost?"

"You're fine, now go!" he demanded.

I put my head down and whispered, "No daddy, it's okay, I'll stay."

He yelled, "I said go! Now get out of here!"

I glanced over at Sam and he looked at his feet. Denise and John Junior quickly climbed back in the car. I searched for Timmy, but he was gone. Did Timmy go to the creek?

An unexplainable sadness overcame me. I felt as if I was again truly alone. "Who will take care of my Sissy and my baby brother?" I said quietly as I hesitantly walked toward the sound of running water. With each step I took away from the camp, I felt like someone took a knife and stabbed me over and over. So many questions ran through my mind and I thought, "I don't hear feet running after me? Don't they realize how much they need me? Why did my father make me go all by myself?" I watched my tears hit the dirt and then told myself, "I can't let them see me cry."

Instantly, Peter was calling out for me, "Come on, Diane, I'll show you the creek! I know about a special place that we can run to!"

As I struggled to keep up with Peter, I yelled, "You're right, Peter, we should hurry. The twins and Little Mother and Crystal and Ruby need me. They will be lost without me!"

Peter looked back at me and chuckled, "Don't worry; I'll bring you to them."

I ran behind Peter repeating, "Are we there yet?" He pointed in the distance and said, "They're over there, Diane!"

I saw my special friends waiting under an old tree. I wrapped my arms around Little Mother's waist and giggled, "It's okay to be lost now, 'cause I'm not alone anymore." I spent the day exploring with them. As the sun set, I sat thinking, "Johnny would really like a friend like Peter. And I know Denise would love to sleep in Little Mother's arms." It made me sad that Johnny and Denise didn't seem to have friends like me. "I hope they find someone safe soon, 'cause I don't want them to ever be lost, 'cause being lost is a bad thing..."

The next day, I woke as the sun peeked through the threads of my tent and to the smell of the morning dew on the trees. It was the barking of my father's cough that reminded me it was time to join my special protectors. I quietly snuck out of camp and soon, I was safe on a branch that hung over the familiar creek.

The day seemed like any other when, suddenly, I heard my father's voice, "I know where you're at so you better high tail it back here!"

I turned to Peter and asked, "What did he say? There's no way he could know our special place." However, the louder his voice became, the more I started to question my safety. I was sure that my father's hands could destroy everything good in one second or less. "If he can see me, then does that mean he can see our hiding place? I don't want him to take it away from me!" I whispered to Peter. Unexpectedly, I felt my feet pounding the dusty gravel and found myself running back towards camp, believing in my mind that my father could see my every move.

As I pushed my way through the low branches and back into camp, I heard the booming sound of his laugh. "What's so funny?" I asked innocently.

"You are!" He responded. I turned to Sam for a confirmation that my father had finally lost his mind, but, to my surprise, Sam and the rest of my siblings were also laughing. Even as I heard their laughter, my sibling's eyes showed fear. Then my father picked up a switch and hit me. With an evil voice he said, "You have disobeyed me and now you must be punished!"

"Why do they hate me?" I cried to myself. Numbness surrounded me.

My father's voice shouted repeatedly, "Diana, just tell me what rules Denise has broken! Then she will be the one punished, not you!" At this moment, I realized that in order to survive, I must tell on my siblings even for crimes they didn't commit. Then I would be expected to laugh, as another child was being tortured.

My father was now in complete control and even insisted on being called "Master."

The Master sometimes left camp for several days at a time. When he returned, every child was ready to fight for whatever food he brought back. I remember one day, he set a single jar of peanut butter in the middle of us. My father instructed us not to move. I sat with my legs crossed, convinced that perhaps if I obeyed, I might earn a little more food than the rest of the children. But, it never seemed to matter how we sat or what we did, the Master always made the ultimate decision.

My father went to sit in an old lawn chair to light a cigarette and drink his beer. After what seemed like forever he shouted, "Go!" His laugh was loud and evil as we tore each other's clothes trying to reach the treasure. Scratching and punching one another in our attempt to grab as much as we could. Then the game was over. It was time to be invisible again. Each of us scrambled away from the laughter of the Master.

When everything settled down, I recalled John Junior didn't fight. He sat still and looked down at his knees as if nothing had happened and there was no need to fight. Timmy had a smudge of peanut butter on an old rusty spoon hidden under his shirt. I watched him lift John Junior's head and then point to the tent. I was shocked to see Timmy slip John Junior the spoon.

"I wish Timmy would be that nice to me," I whispered. I kicked the dirt and trudged into the woods toward the sound of Little Mother's voice.

Soon I sat with Peter picking up blades of grass, putting them to my mouth and attempting to make a whistle sound. I gave up and climbed on the tree to a large limb. I was startled by someone whispering. I looked down and saw two blond heads directly below me! It was Timmy chattering away while Johnny trudged close behind. "How come nobody asked me to play?" I was sure my heart would break when I realized Timmy and Johnny were friends. I struggled to catch my breath as I watched my two brothers walk on toward the creek. They had each other and it seemed as if I had no one. I felt so lonely.

I mumbled, "I must be bad and that's why no one wants to play with me." I looked over to my friend Peter, but he was gone... I wanted to climb down toward my brothers, but, instead, I found myself climbing toward the highest branch. I reached for the black crayon that was always in my pocket and started drawing circles on my shirt. I wrote with the hope of that man, God, rescuing me and making all this hurt go away. I closed my eyes tightly and wished that the black smudges would disappear and somehow my black feelings would disappear too...

The more I thought about it, the madder I got that Timmy and Johnny had actually invaded my space! How dare they walk on my safe place? This is my hideout and my brothers didn't ask if I wanted to share! I felt my face turn red with anger. I mumbled, "Little Mother didn't say it was okay for them to be here!"

Suddenly, the twins, Sue and Dee, appeared and before I knew it, I was slowly moving down the tree. Sue stuttered, "Wait! Can they see me? 'Cause I can see them!"

Dee gasped excitedly, "Maybe if they knew I was here they would ask me to play?" I watched Timmy look with kindness as he helped John Junior onto a muddy cliff.

"Where are they going?" I asked quietly, as I stepped on my tip toes and followed them.

Suddenly Peter cautioned, "Wait! If we are able to follow them, then do you think the Master is following us?" I rolled my eyes and turned away from Peter.

Dee giggled and whispered, "Are they going on a secret adventure? Oh! I wanna go too! This must be a game of Hide and Seek! Maybe when they find us, we

Diana

can laugh and all fall down. Then it will be my turn to hide, just like the games we play with Peter. Yeah, that's it! I just know they'll like me!"

Through the tall grass, I saw my brother's two blonde heads come to a stop, sit down in the sand, and wiggle their feet through the fast moving water. Sue squealed, "Oh, Little Mother, can we go put our feet in the water, too?"

Peter spoke in a deep whisper, "No, we're not invited..." His voice sounded so much like Sam's, I froze and I felt the hair on the back of my neck stand on end! I even turned around to see if it really was Sam, but there was no one with me, not even Peter. When I turned back around, I was face-to-face with Timmy! The look in his eyes told me to run!

"Run, Run! Timmy's gonna get us," the girls giggled as my heart pounded. "If he catches us, we'll lose!" I kept looking back over my shoulder as I ran through the trees, but nobody was coming after me. "Why aren't they chasing me?" Tears fell as I stuttered, "Maybe I'm not worth chasing..."

Dee wrapped her arms around Peter's waist and sobbed, "Why don't they wanna play with me?" I stopped running and stomped my feet in the dirt, "This is no fun..." The black feeling was back and I slowly returned to my safe tree where Ruby and Little Mother sat waiting to comfort us.

It seemed like forever before Timmy's voice faded in the distance. Then I walked down to the creek where my brothers had been playing, plopped down, and put my feet in the water. "This is cold! It's just not fun anymore 'cause I'm all alone... I wish this black feeling would just go away!" I picked up a rock to throw like my brothers had.

I was shocked to see a little blond-haired boy covered with several small cuts. Tears fell down his face and onto his old shirt. Then he sobbed, "Someone, help me!" I'm hurt and can't get up!"

I turned to Little Mother. "Who is this boy and why would he want to hurt himself, Little Mother?"

Then he stuttered, "Cause the crayon didn't work..." and he handed the red rock to Little Mother.

She wrapped her arms around me and him and whispered, "My dear little Diane, don't be mad at him, his name is Willie and he was only trying to make the bad feelings go away. Let's all help this precious child get cleaned up." She scooped some water and rinsed out the cuts. We all sat with our new friend, Willie, and watched the sun go down. Little Mother always has a way of making things better.

Chapter 7

Are You There, God?

The darkening sky was a sign that it would soon be safe enough to return to camp and slip unnoticed into a sleeping bag for the night. However, this night something was different. I caught a wonderfully delicious smell in the air and so I headed back early. I saw my father sitting on his old metal lawn chair. As I passed Timmy, his eyes looked down and I noticed that John Junior was not by his side.

Denise walked past me and asked, "Did you fall? You have some cuts on your legs."

Confused, I answered, "I guess I must have..."

Then, I moved toward the smell and my stomach began to growl. Through the smoke from the campfire I saw a small woman with curly hair talking with Sam. "Is she the same lady that gave me John Junior while we were in the station wagon? She needs to run 'cause the Master won't like her, she looks like me!"

Suddenly, I thought I saw Little Mother standing beside her and Sam. But, as I stepped closer, I saw that it was actually another person making dinner, just a young girl with long black hair. Sam called her

Karen. This girl's eyes told a dark story, one that carried the worries of a grown up and made me afraid. Sam began to talk with her as if he had found an old friend. They talked so fast, and so quiet, as only best friends would.

I heard a voice say, "Oh... my tummy hurts..." I looked down and noticed a little girl tugging at my jeans, not much more than a slight reflection against the darkening sky. "It's me, Shadow, please make the pain go away..." I wrapped my arm around her and she looked up with a slight smile. I wanted so much to talk with Shadow, but that special feeling I got told me she was yet another child that can only be seen by me.

"I must not talk out loud," I thought, "Because Little Mother says there are two worlds that I live in. I think it's sad that my siblings can't see my special friends. Sometimes it's so hard to live in both worlds at the same time. Especially when there's always someone new to meet..."

I went over and sat down thinking to myself, "My father must have brought home some of his women, but who cares, we have real food!"

Then Shadow interrupted, "A woman who can cook! What else could be better?"

The curly-haired lady handed us each a plate with a potato, corn on the cob, and some meat cut up in small pieces. It was strange to have someone care enough to cut my meat. "Did she just smile at us? I wonder why," Peter asked, "And why did she cut up the meat? I'm not a baby!"

Suddenly, my siblings all began to talk with each other while I sat focused on cleaning my plate as fast as I could, so I could be the first to go back for more.

As I jumped up, plate empty, headed for more, Karen slipped up next to me and handed me a fork.

"It is too late for a fork," Shadow laughed, "the food is already gone, and who uses forks anyway?" I was forced to ignore Shadow's comments as the girl's big, dark eyes caught me by surprise. It was as if she was trying to tell me something. It seemed like she knew how to talk with her eyes, just like my siblings and I did when words were not allowed.

Then she whispered, "I am Karen," as though she knew me.

Did she know me? I wondered and I gave her a small smile, all the while questioning her trust. What was she trying to tell me? Was she going to talk to my father like the girl in the motel? Would she cause more trouble for me? I didn't want that because the Master was already mad at me.

Denise pushed her way in between us and wrapped her arms around Karen's waist. I clenched my fists and felt my face turn red as I thought, "How dare she push me away!"

I sat on the ground and began my pouting position. Lip out, and my arms wrapped around me. "Doesn't Denise know she came to me first?" I grumbled to myself, "So she's my friend now!" I even made a small sound (as if I was crying), but no matter how much I whined, Karen didn't seem to notice and kept talking with Denise. Obviously in this situation, I needed to go to drastic measures, so I jumped up, walked over and pushed my twin down! Denise needed to be reminded of the rules, so I blurted out, "She is my new friend 'cause she talked to me first!" Denise glared at me, crossed her arms, flipped her blond hair and turned away. I was sure I had won as Karen turned to me with a smile and said, "You remember me?"

I tossed a victory glance at Denise and I said to Karen, "Sure, I remember you..."

Diana

As soon as I said it, I felt my legs start to shake and I quietly whispered to myself, "Did I really know her?" So many unseen voices came all at once that I walked away to find some safety in my tent. I grabbed a blanket and dragged myself back near the campfire where my brothers and sisters were still talking with each other.

"What's going on?" I asked out loud.

Denise looked at me with a growl, "You're stupid!"

I wanted to belt her one, when Karen stopped me and said, "You two need to stop fighting and listen to me because I am your big sister!"

Her voice sounded as if she was now in charge, but then I paused and thought, "Yeah, right, that's what all the girls at the motel said. I just turned seven, and I know that nobody's really who they say they are."

At the sound of the car engine starting, my siblings suddenly got quiet. We all looked at each other and realized the adults were gone! I wondered if this time was the last I would see the Master and his new lady... Peter said, "Whew! They're gone!"

"But," Shadow said, "What if they don't come back? How will we eat?"

Those thoughts of worry were replaced by feelings of great sadness as I heard my brother Sam and big sister Karen laughing and talking like true siblings. I reflected back to Timmy and John Junior's closeness together under my tree. My heart continued to ache as I saw Denise scoot close to Karen. Karen then wrapped her arm around Denise, and my twin snuggled in closer, as Sam continued to talk. I wanted so badly to walk up to everyone, but each step I took was only another step away from the children who were supposed to be my family.

"I really want to go sit with them." Sue pleaded.

"What's wrong with us?" sobbed Dee.

"Why can't we move the body closer to the fire? Are we going to get hurt?" Willie asked with his quiet voice.

I remembered when we used to play games like Jacks with the siblings. Now, when we're near them, I felt as if I couldn't breathe. Even when the man who had so much control over our every move was not here to stop us... There is nothing that makes it safe to be with them now. It seems as if I'm hurting even when I should be happy.

A deep, steady voice said firmly, "Diane, Peter, it's time to get these children away from the fire, Little Mother is waiting." We all turned and saw a figure of a young woman wearing a long dark robe.

My voice trembled as I asked, "Who are you?"

She answered, "My name is Midnight, you need not be afraid of me, for I am here to protect you. We all share one body and I will protect you from those it's safe to see and those you're not prepared to meet yet."

"You mean there're more children like us?" asked Peter.

Midnight responded, "Yes, Peter, they are much younger than you, and I will decide when the time is right for you to meet them. Little Mother and I believe that some decisions are too big for one person to make alone."

Midnight faded into the darkness as Ruby met us at the flap of the tent. I could hear Karen and Sam still talking in the distance. John Junior somehow reached the tent before me and was already sleeping. I looked over at him, and attempted to ignore the pain that was still in my heart. The blankets were warm as I snuggled into them and I could feel my special book underneath my pillow. Little Mother held me as I dozed off to sleep. I felt such comfort as I heard her humming me to sleep, and felt her hands push my hair away from my face. I am so glad I have my Little Mother. She will never leave us.

I woke up to the sun peeking through the seams of the tent, got up, and went out to the remains of last night's fire. I thought I was alone, but suddenly found myself face-to-face with the curly-haired lady.

I decided to ask her, "How do you know my father, anyway?"

She responded, "I'm your mother."

I thought to myself, "Okay, I'll go along with this game. She's not the first girl my father has brought here that said she was my mother, although he does seem to act differently around her... It's as if she's the boss."

"My name is 'Deborah,'" she finished. She looked at me as if she expected me to jump for joy, and wrap my arms around her.

"What did you just say?" I said out loud. That horrible name caused such fear that my heart began to pound faster than ever before. My face turned red with anger and I clenched my fists. Just then I saw my father struggling to get out of the tent that they were sharing. The look in his eyes told me this feeling of rage was unacceptable.

Peter yelled, "Run!"

I ran toward the trees and began to scream out to God, "Are you there, God?!? The girl at the motel said you are stronger than anyone. Please hear me! Please let my legs run forever!" Immediately, my legs went faster! However, with each step I was sure I could feel some large rough hands tearing at my clothes. I could even hear the heavy breathing. I must not have been moving fast enough! I was terrified to look behind me; I needed to get to my safe place before it was too late. I needed to escape to the tree!

"No time to think, just run!" Peter kept repeating, "If we just keep running, no one can catch us!" I just kept hearing so many screams, some I recognized and some I didn't!

"Ruby! Help me! The Master has already ruined my pink skirt and now this monster is going to hurt me, too! You said you'd come and take my place when the pain is too much. Where are you?!?" I frantically yelled. "I just need to get to my safe place. Then Ruby, Little Mother, and everybody will protect me from the scary monsters that are chasing me!"

"Run, Peter, I see the tree! We're almost there!" I screamed as I tried to catch my breath. When I reached the tree, I snapped at Ruby, "Why didn't you come like you promised?"

Ruby calmly replied, "Why would I come? You look okay to me. I see no cuts and it does not look like you've been hurt. I will always keep my promise."

"But, Ruby, nobody's helping me... Not even you... Did I do something so bad that you wouldn't come when I called?"

"Diane," she said with a firm voice, "My blanket of protection will not help you this time; the pain you feel is not on your body, but in your heart." Ruby placed her hand on my shoulder and said, "Look behind you, my child, there are no monsters chasing you. I promised that I would give you a band-aid if you had a cut, but I don't see any."

I looked down at my body and saw no red stains...

My world began to spin as I cried, "But! But! Help me, someone help me..."

I stumbled to the ground as the many faces of my protectors started circling around me. I clung to Ruby's dark eyes and her familiar, bright red lipstick, but could no longer make any sense of what she was saying...

Slowly, each unseen child dropped to the grass and snuggled close beside me. Ruby joined us and her reassuring eyes and comforting voice helped me to finally breathe. She may not have used her blanket this time, but I knew somewhere deep inside that she had kept her promise. I asked one more time, "But if it's not a monster, then who's chasing me and why does it hurt so bad?"

Ruby simply said, "Shh, shh... Little Mother is who you need now."

I put my head on Little Mother's lap. "It's okay," Little Mother reminded me. Her arms reached out and pulled me close.

The world started going black as I closed my eyes. "I'm so tired of running, Little Mother, when will it ever stop?"

Little Mother paused for a short time, and responded in her soft voice, "Someday... Just stay strong, keep writing, and someone will hear your cry and make the monsters go away. Someday..."

As Little Mother's voice faded, Midnight's voice took over, "Diane, you can't stay in the darkness too long. The ones that stand here in the dark next to me must hide behind me until I decide it's safe. You need to get up and be seen."

Then all went silent and the only sound I heard was my own breathing. "Am I sleeping? Am I awake? Where am I?" I asked in a hushed voice.

A light appeared, like a tiny star in the distance. Before I was able to say another word, the light revealed Crystal, dancing and giggling in her pretty pink skirt. As I moved away from Midnight, I could also hear Sue and Dee giggling. Then Peter reached for my hand and said, "Come on, let's go play."

I could feel the warm sun on my face as Willie handed me his stick and said, "Lift me up on the tree branch; I want to play, too." I started to laugh as Willie's rocks fell out of his pocket when he reached for the highest limb.

Then suddenly I heard a voice in the distance, "Diana, obey your mother and get back to camp, now!"

At the very sound of her voice, my hands tightened into a fist. "She is not my mother," a voice muttered.

"Don't worry, she won't find us here," Peter interrupted. With those reassuring words, Willie and I continued to sit on the limb, watching our legs swing beneath us.

"But wait," Peter paused with concern, "if we stay here, we may lose our safe spot, and never be able to return. She may be like the Master and take away all the good things. We'd better go..."

I grumbled as I climbed down the tree, and stomped toward the angry voice, my heart pounded louder with every step. I angrily rubbed the sweat from my stinging eyes, and wiped it roughly on my clothes.

I was so focused on my dirty feet kicking the dust, that it completely shocked me when I found myself facing this woman who called herself my mother. It was almost as if I was looking at my own reflection. Her dark, curly hair and black eyes made me scream, "She is my mother!"

I trembled as I could hear the monsters rushing towards me. We all wanted to run, but one angry voice declared, "I'm not running! She doesn't scare me!" I looked beside me and met the fiery, black eyes of Deanna. "We must be strong; we cannot let that woman see us cry," she stated.

"But, Deanna, every time I hear the word 'mother' the monsters start chasing me."

Peter said, "You're right, Diane! She must've brought them with her. I'll bet they were hiding in the back seat of her car!"

Deanna responded, "Then we have to make her go away. Only then will we be safe, because the monsters will go away, too."

Then, she brushed away her frizzy, blond curls and flopped her arm over my shoulder. "You watch me, I will get her monsters, they won't get me!" I felt her strength as my own and it gave me the courage to keep walking. Even though Deanna made me feel better, I still knew the monsters were hiding in the trees, waiting...

Chapter 8

The Fire

When we got back to camp, the woman ordered, "You get to bed! I don't want to hear any more out of you today."

Then Deanna said to me, "Who does she think she is, tellin' us what to do?!?" I then nodded my head in agreement. As I stomped my feet towards the tent, making sure everyone knew Deborah didn't scare me, I was startled to hear Deanna mumble, "Although, I am really sleepy..."

It wasn't all that long, maybe just a few days, before I had to admit that this lady did make life safer. She seemed to be the only one who could cool the fury in my father's eyes. Only her voice could send him into fits of laughter.

Sue and Dee even asked if it would be okay to call her mother. Peter responded, "She will never be our Little Mother, but we can call her Mom. After all, she does keep the Master away."

One early morning, I woke to the shock of an icy rag wiping my eyes. I could hear the cold wind whistling through the tent, and I could feel the damp wet blankets around me. I swiped at the rag and snapped, "Get it off of me!"

Then Karen whispered, "Shhh, you need to be quiet and stay here in the tent, dad will find out you have this and then we'll all be in trouble! Mom says its pink eye, don't touch your eyes."

I pushed her hands away because I couldn't resist the strong urge to scratch them. But the more I rubbed my eyes, the harder it was to see. So I obeyed Karen and stayed hidden in the tent as long as I could.

I thought I might be the only one who was sick, but soon I recognized the moaning and crying of my brothers and sister lying around me. Through the haze, my eyes strained to watch Karen as she tripped over the tangled blankets. I had forgotten what life was like without her.

As I struggled to find comfort in my, now wet, pillow, Shadow whined, "Diane, please tell Little Mother my eyes itch and I don't feel so good..."

Sue and Dee began to cry, "Me, too!" Then I felt someone put their arms gently around me. At first I wasn't sure whether it was Little Mother or Karen, because now it seemed they could both make things all better. In their arms, I felt safe and my body could lose the stiffness I didn't even realize was there. This time it was Karen and she said, "Try to get some sleep."

I drifted in and out of sleep and it felt like hours had passed before I woke up again. Denise, John Junior, and I were still lying in the same wet blankets. I rubbed the crust from my eyes and life was still a fog. I couldn't believe my brothers and sister were sleeping through all the yelling that was going on outside. I tried to lift my weak body to look out of the tent flap and strained my eyes to see the light of the fire. I could see that Mom was really angry at my father. She grabbed her purse and stumbled toward her car. Peter said knowingly, "Oh, she's been drinking like the master, that's why she's so mad."

As she approached the car door, my father grabbed her arm. She turned and smacked him several times, and screamed lots of words we weren't allowed to say. I thought for sure she was gonna be in trouble for talking to him like that. Instead, he backed away!

I heard Deanna gasp, "Did you see that?!?"

Peter said, "She must be even stronger than him!"

My eyes stung but I forced myself to continue to watch. As she sped away, leaving only an echo of the engine, I was sure I saw my father crying. He just stood still, wiped his eyes, and continued looking down.

I was so busy watching my father, that it startled me when I heard a soft crying sound. Peter pointed outside the tent and whispered, "I think its Karen." I looked where Peter was pointing and saw Karen's small body curled up all alone behind the tent.

Sue began to cry, "I don't like that sound, it hurts my heart."

Willie added, "Hold me, I'm afraid."

Suddenly, a sharp pain shot through my chest and I realized, "It hurts more to see someone I love cry, than to cry myself."

Peter muttered, "Her mother must have forgotten to take her. Oh, no! Now the father can get her, too..."

Sue asked, "Why did her mom leave her? How long has she been crying?"

Dee then asked, "What's wrong with Deanna? Even she is crying..."

I looked towards Deanna and all I saw was a single tear falling down her cheek. Willie moved over next to where Deanna was sitting and held her. Deanna continued to stay stiff, as Willie draped his arms over her shoulders, buried his face in her hair and started to cry. The air felt so heavy, it was as if we were at a funeral and someone had actually died. But there was nobody to explain our feeling of loss.

Deanna jumped up and stomped her foot and said under her breath, "If anyone wants to hurt the siblings, they're gonna have to go through me first! It's okay if they hurt me, but it's not okay to hurt the siblings." Deanna started pacing back and forth while she kept piercing her leg with a stick and said, "I knew it! Karen is staying in the mother's shadow and just waiting for her to return. And, even if she does come back, who's to say she won't leave again... maybe, then, Karen will be left all alone in an even scarier place."

I thought to myself, "Is this woman so powerful that she could actually make Karen die by leaving?"

Deanna continued, "That's never gonna happen to me! I'm never gonna have a parent..."

Sue asked, "Why can't we love someone, Deanna? Is it really that bad?"

Deanna snapped, "Don't you see? We can't because, staying in the shadows is really bad, but waiting for someone to come back and get you could cause you to die!"

Little Mother interrupted, "Now that's enough. Deanna, you're scaring the kids. We all need to get to bed."

After a few days, our eyes became so swollen it was hard to see. My father's shadow paced back and forth around the light of the fire. Panic was in the air. His shadow was moving toward my brother's tent. He yelled up into the dark sky, as his cigarette hung from his lip. He stumbled around, out of control. Timmy was the first to be pulled out of the tent by my father. I attempted to focus my eyes, as each child was yanked out of their beds and beaten. Due to the illness, we were blind and helpless. It seemed like as soon as one of us fell to the ground, he would start to swing his fists until we could no longer see through our swollen eyes.

I heard Karen scream, "Stop Daddy, what did we do?" Doesn't she know you don't question the Master? This must be the first time she's seen him without the woman around.

The Master demanded we all form a line. We could feel each others' bare bodies as we struggled to stand up straight. I felt a cold shoulder on each side of me, and I could hear my brothers and sisters struggling to hold back the tears. His large body started pacing back and forth again. I could smell the smoke from his cigarette as he marched past my face. He yelled, "I want to know who started this illness? All of you will stand here through the night until someone tells me." It was quiet until he shouted, "Okay! I will start at the end of the line, and each child will get back-handed until one of you confesses."

Denise was the first to scream in pain, then I heard one of my brothers say, "Denise didn't do it, I did!"

I heard my father begin beating the child who had confessed. I thought surely it was my older brother, Sam. I remembered Sam, and how mangled his body was the day he first fought for me. I held my breath, and assumed I was next.

Karen then yelled, "Daddy, please stop! Timmy didn't mean to do it."

My heart stopped pounding for a moment. Did she just say Timmy? But Timmy always gets away...

I tried so hard to rub the fog from my eyes and I caught just a glimpse, "It is Timmy! Timmy is taking the beating for us all!" I could clearly hear his bare body being hit several times with a belt. With each snap my body cringed, until the Master ordered us all to bed. As Karen took my hand and guided me back to the tent, I heard the Master say, "Timmy, not you, I'm not done with you yet." I went to sleep knowing Timmy paid the price for something none of us did.

As the early morning sun shone through the openings in our tent, I felt the cold wind against my face. I felt my brother, John Junior, beginning to snuggle even closer to me in an attempt to stay warm. The weight of his arms around my stomach reminded me of the abuse from the night before. I strained to lift my head, and climb out of the sleeping bags and blankets. The cold air and the soreness shot pain throughout my entire body.

Peter asked, "I wonder where Timmy is? I wonder if he kicked the Master really good last night."

Deanna added, "I would've. I would've kicked him real hard."

My eyes filled with a cloud of film that I struggled to wipe clean. Karen whispered with a stern voice, "I've already told you several times not to rub it, it will only make it worse and then daddy will punish us again today."

I noticed she was already up and dressed in many layers of clothing. Karen had firmly taken the position of boss in our family, and Sam no longer cared to fight for that spot. She had a wet cloth, and began to rub my eyes repeatedly, until I pulled away.

"I can see better now," Deanna snapped at her, "I can take care of myself."

Willie jumped in with, "Deanna, that's not very nice to say."

The twins, Sue and Dee, agreed with Willie...

Peter said, "Now, c'mon guys, maybe we can have more than one mother, but Little Mother will always be our real mom."

I added, "After all, even though Karen can be a little bossy, her eyes show how much she loves us all."

I worked my way to the opening of the tent, all the while reaching for shirts and blankets to wrap around my body. I quietly stepped into the cold wind. It appeared to be getting colder every day. As I approached the circle of ashes from the fire, my body began to shake. I gathered a few branches, and attempted to drag a heavy log to the circle and realized I needed someone to help me. My body was so small, and such a heavy task made me fall helplessly on the ground.

Just as I was about to retreat to my tent to get warm, I heard someone wrestling with the opening of my father's tent. And, as I began my escape, I looked behind me and saw Timmy.

Peter said, "Wait, was he sleeping in the Master's tent? Or, is it Sam's tent? Yep, I'm sure that's it. He always sleeps in Sam's tent."

Willie asked, "I wonder if he's okay?"

Deanna said, "Of course he is, I'm sure Timmy is stronger than the Master. But, we probably shouldn't ask any questions."

Willie responded, "But he looks really hurt."

I said, "Hey, let's just ask Timmy to help us get the fire started." I turned to Timmy and asked, "Timmy, can you help me start the fire?"

He nodded his head and moved toward the sticks. I felt a deep sorrow for my brother that morning. As I stood behind the tent and watched him start the fire, I could see the stiffness in his body as he bent down. I tried to erase from my mind the weeping and pain that I heard through the night. I wanted to believe everyone was going to be okay. I wanted to know Timmy didn't continue to be hurt again through the night as we slept.

I moved and sat on a rock behind the tent, attempting to be invisible. I heard someone laughing, and smoke came from all directions! I said, "Is that the Master laughing so loud? And where did all the smoke come from?" I was choking as I came around the tent. I could not believe what I was seeing! It was not my father laughing, but Timmy! The flames were higher than I have ever seen them. It looked as if my brother had gone insane. I suddenly realized that Timmy would never be invisible again. Timmy had just found his way to be seen. Through the flashes of flames, I felt a relief that usually only occurred at my tree, near the creek. Timmy and I looked at each other and I instantly knew that, no matter what the Master did to us, he could never break the siblings apart. The rest of my brothers and sisters came stumbling out of their tents, rubbing their eyes and coughing.

Sam yelled, "Quick, everybody, stomp out those flames, they're starting to spread all over the camp!"

We all giggled, but Timmy was uncontrollable, as he laughed and ran around the flames.

I heard the Master yelling profanities as he forced his body out of his tent. The look of fear grew in my father's eyes as he watched Timmy putting more wood onto the flames. Perhaps my brother had found a doorway to my father's weakness. It was obvious that Timmy was now in control of my father. He could not get to Timmy to abuse him through the flames that stood between them.

I was startled by the mild tone in my father's voice as he instructed, "Take those pots to the creek, fill

Timmy

them up and put out this fire." We all ran to the creek to bring back pots full of water. Everybody exchanged knowing looks and snickers under our breath as we passed each other on the path. All except Timmy who laughed out loud as he ran off into the woods. As the last of the flames were doused, no one spoke. Smoke and ashes were everywhere. We all watched as my father stood still. His face was white as he struggled to catch his breath. "It's time to pack, kids," he said as he walked away. I felt no need to ask Timmy for any more help.

Rain fell throughout the day. We all stomped in mud, as we packed up our belongings, most of which carried a strong odor of smoke. The small amount of food that was left tasted like ashes. We communicated with few words, as each item was stuffed in the back of the old car. This car became our home again. I felt some loss, leaving behind the special memories of my safe tree and the peaceful sound of the bubbling creek.

The roar of an engine coming up the dirt road interrupted my reflections of my time in camp. My mother's car came to a slippery stop, as more mud flew onto her car.

Peter warned, "That woman is back. Quick, run to the tree!"

"No!" Deanna argued, "We don't need to run anymore. She doesn't scare me!" Then Deanna clenched her fists and stuffed them into her pockets.

As soon as the woman stepped out of the car, she ordered, "Put some of that stuff in this car." Denise and John Junior obediently picked up some blankets and walked toward her car.

I put my arm around Deanna's shoulder and said, "Never mind her, let's just finish packing."

Deanna said, "Okay, but I'm not riding with her!"

Once the cars were full, my father demanded, "Everybody load up, it's time to hit the road." For some strange reason, all the other siblings chose to ride with my mother while I climbed into the car with my father. Don't they realize the power she has?

My mother's car pulled out first, and we followed in her taillights. I sat quietly in the back seat as my father yelled, "Who does she think she is!" Just as I started to answer his question like I'd been trained to, he answered the question himself. It was as if I wasn't even there as he continued to swear about her.

Peter said, "He doesn't even know you're here, he thinks you're the mother. C'mon, let's just get under the blankets."

Sue and Dee rubbed their eyes and fought over whose pillow was whose.

The Master startled us all by yelling out, "Deborah!"

In an instant, I looked over and Crystal was sitting with me in her pretty pink skirt. She didn't seem to be bothered by that name. He shouted, "Deborah," again. This time I felt Ruby's arms around me and she assured me, "Little one, remember I'm here whenever you need me."

I replied, "But, Ruby, I'm scared. Every time he says her name, bad things happen to me."

Deanna said, "There are more of us than there are of them. Don't worry; I'll make sure that we're okay." It was not long before my father's voice was now just a mumbled sound that mixed with the engine. Then I looked over and saw Little Mother smiling at me gently as Shadow, the twins, and little Willie snuggled close to her.

As I laid my aching body down on Little Mother's lap, I still felt a loneliness I didn't understand. Tears began to fill my eyes. Why was I so different? How

Diana

come I had to live in three worlds? My siblings and I lived together in the world we were born into. Why wasn't it okay for me to stay there? And I didn't know why they couldn't see Peter and the rest of us here in this world. And then there was that really scary third world that always came when the mother's name was mentioned, where even my siblings and my protectors couldn't go. Without my siblings and Ruby, Little Mother, Peter, Deanna, and the rest, I feared I might die.

My body trembled at the thought of being in a world where I was all alone and the monsters were chasing me. Was there anyone out there who could fill this empty feeling? Suddenly, I remembered that the girl in the motel said the man named God could do anything. All I had to do was ask Him. My voice shook as I whispered, "God, are you there? Can you hear me? I can't feel you. I can't see you. I can't hear you. But the girl in the motel said you were there. You have to be there God, I need you! God, you are my only hope to escape the hole I feel within me! Please tell me which world you are in. I will go there and you can save me."

As I type these words down, I already know the answer. I can feel God's presence and hear Him tell me, "I was with you from the very beginning, sitting in the chair... And I walked with you through each chapter of your life. Now I'm sitting here with you today. I have never left you. 'I will never leave you nor forsake you, my child. (Joshua 1:5)'" I slowly close the cover on the last of my childhood journals and return to the reality that my life is not exactly what I wanted it to be, but it is what it is. I know the scars will always be with me. Here on earth, they will never be erased. But, I no longer need to wear a mask. The true story is out and, in the end, that's all that really matters. I pray that these pages I've written will open a doorway that gives my siblings and me permission to heal. I may find the ability to write more of my story in the future, but for now I will end this book with the present and the hope that it may bring to those who read it.

Chapter 9

Forgiven

My hands trembled and tears fell on the keyboard as I closed this chapter of my life. I wept for all the many years we lost. I wish I could tell you that the abuse ended there, but the truth is that it continued for many more years and in even more terrifying ways. My heart aches at the reality that it wasn't long after this point in our lives, that we had no control over with who and where we would live.

My brothers were separated from us when I was eight, and it was several years before I was able to see them again. They occasionally reappeared while fleeing from my father, only to discover that the situation my sisters and I were in was even worse. The men they forced us to call 'Father' did not accept any boys in our lives, including our own brothers.

At such a young age, each of us was already being molded into who we are today. I truly believe we could have been helped, but we never had the chance as children to see the world differently. It was only after we reached adulthood, and the world gave us our freedom, that we felt safe enough to explore our own identities. At the beginning of this book, I wrote an open letter to my siblings. To end this book, I will let each one of them know how much I love them and will never forget the love we shared and the commitment each of them had to me, despite my dissociation from the world we lived in.

My dear sister Karen,

I'm so sorry you had to carry the worries of a mother of five small helpless children at such a young age. Your love for all of us was, and is, endless. It didn't surprise me when you graduated from nursing school as a single mother with two small children of your own. I remember the nights you cared for me and refused to leave me sick and alone. I hear your shaky voice, "But Diana is still sick....she won't stop throwing up....isn't there something we can do?" To this day I can hear the worry in your voice as you ask, "Diana, how are you feeling?" With those words I'm reminded that now you are not only a nurse to your siblings, but you share that gift with many others. Karen, please don't blame yourself for the abuse we all experienced. I don't care what our father told us the rules were. Just because you were the oldest doesn't mean you could have stopped it. I want you to know how thankful I am that God gave me such a strong sister who would never give up caring for her siblings.

And now I write to my oldest brother Sam,

You also took on the position as parent in our family. You not only took care of us, but you took care of our father. So many days I watched you jump at our father's every command. I know that it was your way of protecting us from his unpredictable wrath. I will never forget the sacrifices you made for me, my dear brother. You never forgot me when I thought I was invisible. You are so wise beyond your years and your courage and strength is what kept us together when we were young. Your gentle smile always had a way of making the bad things in life seem better. You are more of a man than our father ever was and you are truly my hero.

To my brave brother Timmy,

You weren't afraid to express the anger we all felt towards our father. Even as a child, you held such a strong will. You had the will to fight for your littlest brother, as well as for all of us. Timmy, you always seemed to know just when to stay hidden and when to sacrifice yourself to make sure we were all seen. You learned at an early age what our father's weaknesses were and used them against him to protect us. Your bold sense of humor could get us all laughing in the toughest of times. I admire the fact that, even when you were hurting, you always stayed strong for us. To this day, every phone call ends with, "Diana, you know I love you, don't you?" You never needed to say you loved me, I could always tell by your actions. But, "Yes, Timmy, I love you too."

To my baby brother John Junior,

I regret the fact that, out of all the siblings, it is you who I still long to see today. I never had the opportunity to see you grow from the age of seven into your adulthood. The youngest of six siblings, you remained unseen. Tears fell from my eyes when I checked the book orders and your name and phone number were on the list. I picked up the phone and my hands shook as I dialed your number and a deep voice answered. It was nice to finally have the chance to talk with you and I can't believe you told me you're now over six feet tall. I want you to know, John Junior, this book was also written for you, the one child I lost so many years ago. It is my prayer that, through this book, you and I will finally meet. I hope that you will read this letter and know how much I love you and miss you. Every time I see a little blond-haired boy, I am reminded of my special baby brother, the one who let me be bigger than him.

My friend... My twin sister,

Growing up I believed that there was no need to use words to tell you what I was feeling. Mainly because it has always felt as if you were half of me and so no words were necessary. Adults told us that before we were old enough to walk, we had our own language, and that the words we spoke were ones that only the two of us understood. To this day, no matter how many miles lay between us, our silent language still exists. Over the last five years, as I have struggled through this book, I realize you too have been carrying some of the pain with me.

I remember a day when I thought the pain was too deep and I couldn't type another word... you called and, through your tears, I realized that I must continue. You hold a place in my heart that was created just for you, the kind only twins share. It was always you and me against the world.

Those words you said over the phone, "Diana, I want you to know I tried to stop them," have given me the strength every day to finish this book. When my head hits the pillow every night a prayer is always whispered for your safety. There were years in which the pain from our childhood kept us running away *from each other instead of running towards my closest friend... my twin sister. All of us took different paths in order to survive... you my twin show in your eyes that you continue to cry for the burdens we all suffered. Denise, there is no need for you to carry all the worries; it is time for each sibling to find our own path to healing. Thank you for your tender heart and your unending support. I hope you know how beautiful you are to me. Together we are one and you complete me.*

And, as for me...

I worked really hard to forget the life I lived as a child. I married a wonderful man and gave birth to three beautiful children. My husband and I also chose to adopt five 'special needs' children, not to mention the many others we cared for through the foster system. I worked in the social care industry and even went on the speaking circuit, teaching and training in the area of childhood development. I had very little connection with my mother and siblings and no contact with my father. I did hear that he was incarcerated on and off for his crimes and that he died somewhere, in the late 1990's. I truly believed that, through my physical health challenges and years of therapy as an adult, I had faced all the fears that life had thrown at me. Everything was going pretty smoothly until September 11, 2003. The day my foster children were taken away. That was the day Social Services used a diagnosis of Multiple Personalities Disorder (MPD) to accuse me of being an unfit parent.

When I sat down and starting writing to defend myself and my family against the accusations, I had no idea what was true. I simply could not believe the diagnosis was real. I was sure they had the wrong person and had made a serious mistake. I went to the only resource I could trust, my closest Christian friend, Rhonda. She gently reminded me that God was in control, and all I needed to do was be obedient to Him.

From that time on, my bible has been by my side throughout this entire process. God knows the beginning and the end. He turned something horrible into something beautiful. It was only through each journal, that I discovered the answers that led to my healing. With each new page, I was re-introduced to another personality. Each face reminded me of the incredible task that God had assigned them. This awareness caused me to realize my biggest fear that someone might actually see me as mentally ill, even though to me it was God's greatest gift of protection for my survival.

I was suddenly experiencing the truth that many personalities share this one body, and that to protect the body, we must act like one on the outside, so we can fit in and not appear different. My hands trembled on the keyboard as I realized that the rule that I always had to live by still exists today. We must act as one in order to be what society calls "normal."

If I'm "normal," then it is acceptable to be a mother, work with children, and be successful. Now I know that society doesn't see what I was experiencing inside myself. I have no need to apologize to the world for labels that have been put upon me. I am just a person with gifts and challenges like everybody else. I am a good mother, a happy wife, a successful woman, and, now, I am an author of an important healing book.

As I said in chapter one, my oldest daughter also played a powerful role in my ability to accept myself and others. I marvel at how God still uses her to this day. When I see her and her children, I rejoice at the fact that life is about growth and change. Just last year, at her twin boy's birthday party, she turned to me for the first time and actually called me "Mom." A deep part of me healed when I heard those loving words. My oldest daughter has taught me the greatest lesson of all. One that God Himself lived. That is, "Do not judge, and you will not be judged. Do not condemn, and you will not be condemned. Forgive, and you will be forgiven. *(Luke 6:37)*" I am humbled by her commitment to loving me unconditionally, even when I didn't love myself. She was able to break down the walls of defense that had been built by years of judgment, anger, and resentment.

This brings me to my thoughts about my own mother... I judged her based on the many stories my father told me. I wish I would have looked into her eyes and seen that her actions, like all of us, were based on survival. Perhaps her behaviors were a reaction to some past abuse? Was she forced to leave us? How did she come to the point of living with horrible men like my father? Those questions are not mine to answer. The lesson I have learned is to not judge, but to forgive her and see who she is today. "Get rid of all bitterness, rage and anger, brawling and slander, along with every form of malice. Be kind and compassionate to one another, forgiving each other, just as in Christ, God forgave you. *(Ephesians 4:31-32)*"

Recently, she and I met at the airport, while she was returning home from her mother's funeral. She only had a short layover and requested that I meet her there. As I sat with her and we picked at our plates of airport food, we started to talk like never before. It became immediately obvious that we both

had changed, though I'm not sure when or where. Maybe it was that she had just lost her mother, maybe it was that I finally understood myself? We may never know... Suddenly, she glanced at me then looked down quickly and opened her suitcase. Hiding her tears, she gently pulled out a carefully wrapped bible and turned her face away as she handed it to me. She quietly whispered, "This belonged to your Grandmother, she wanted you to have it." I gasped as I reached for the precious gift that symbolized the truth that my life had finally come full circle. The tension in my body washed away as I put my head into her shoulder and said, "I love you, Mom."

She kissed me on the cheek and whispered in my ear, "I love you too, dear." As we embraced each other and cried openly, I knew all was forgiven.

Today, after many years of individual searching, it has become clear to me that no one of us, including my own mother, carried more guilt than the other. The wounds are the same. It is just that each of us learned to cope with life differently. Some of us found healing through the eyes of our own children. And for some, the path of healing was to never look back. It is my heartfelt prayer that all who find themselves reading this book will be blessed with healing, just as I have been while writing it.

I think it's obvious why I have a passion for children and, to this day, I still cry deep within every time I'm triggered by the sights and sounds of a child suffering. It just takes one word, or the presence of an unknown memory, or the look into the eyes of a hurting child, and I flashback to a smoke-filled room and the angry eyes of my father as I sit in the big chair. It has taken me a long time to understand the flashbacks. I must move through them in order to help someone else in need. I use the Bible's promises to find strength and courage to continue. God's Word says, "Do not be anxious about anything, but in everything, by prayer and petition, with thanksgiving, present your requests to God. And the peace of God, which transcends all understanding, will guard your hearts and your minds in Christ Jesus. *(Philippians 4:6-7)*" My hope is that you, too, can learn to go on and use your life experiences to help the hurting and unseen children of today.

Now it's time to turn the page and read the poetry, journals, and see the art that was painfully written by other unseen children from all over the world. Contributions come from my own daughters on the day the foster children were taken away and they felt unseen, some come from those I have foster-parented personally, and others simply heard of the promise and sent their stories in the hopes of finally being seen.

These poems and stories in "Book Two" have been collected over time, and for a few, who are now older, the cycle continues. One is now in prison, and some have lost their rights to parent, however, most are very successful in breaking the old patterns that trapped them as children. There is also a brave young lady who has stirred my heart for years with her persistence in fighting a terminal disease, all with the hope of handing this book on to her own daughter.

Please, we all ask you, as you live and work among the children of today, look into their eyes and help them let go of the guilt they are carrying. I pray that, together, we can put a stop to the cycle of abuse.

BOOK TWO

the unseen children of today...

On That Day
by Alyssa

On that day.
The day they took part of my family away.
Maybe yes? Maybe no?
What to think I didn't know?

I saw my mom cry.
The whole room was a blur,
as I watched them pack.
I wondered if they would ever be back.

Tears began to grow in my eyes
as I heard my sisters say good-bye.
I began to cry, and scream.

I thought to myself, "Why didn't they think of us?"
The tears and heartaches in me
wanted to hurt them all.
But, I knew the rules.

The tears poured out more and more
as I watched them get in cars.
They told me I had to watch them go.

The words stung like bees
that kept stinging me over and over again.
Then I realized I couldn't do anything,
because I was the one who they didn't see.

Never Alone
by a twelve-year-old girl

Have you ever felt alone?
Always knocking on doors but no one's ever home.

Have you ever ran away,
just to escape the light of day?

There's no one to catch you,
No superman to save you.

Have you ever cried away your fears?
Searched for someone to wipe your tears?

Have you ever felt like there's no place for you?
No life for you.

You're just there,
floating in air,
and no one ever cared.

But just know
you're not alone.

When the faster kids went
away all I could remember
was that I was scared, scared
of what might happen next,
scared of — that spider,
in the web, and scared
because Carl is scared, so scared.
a suit

Dex

Help me God
by a small child of thirteen

Help me God my fathers back.
What am I supposed to do?
What am I supposed to say?
I only told the truth of the pain
that he caused on those nights long ago,
How did he get out of the bars
that were meant to protect me?

At night I see him,
At night I hear him,
Why did I tell them?
Nothing can make him go away?
Help me God!

The people I trusted told me I would be safe.
The promise was broken.
Help me God, my fathers back.
What am I supposed to do?
What am I supposed to say?

At night I wake up there is wetness all around me?
That's when I know he's back!
Will the bars ever protect me?
Will I always wake up wet?
Help me God!
Make him go away,
Promise me God.

Safe Place
by Chanel

Just our luck, we had no place to go. We were living with a friend of my mom's, when an argument occurred and we were asked to leave her home even though she knew we had court the next day.

We started the search for a place to stay in a shelter. We went to many of them, but each place told us "No" for various reasons. As we left the last shelter with no other options, the night had become cold and rainy. We reluctantly drove to my grandparent's and parked in front of the house. My mom didn't want to go in and be confronted for not providing a safe environment.

Due to no help from the system, or anyone who saw my mom and me helplessly driving in the night, we were forced to sleep in our station wagon. All I can remember was how cold it was outside as my body shivered and I tossed and turned through the night until morning approached.

It was cold and misty that morning when we woke up to attend the court hearing for my older sister. The first question they asked my mom was, "Do you have permanent and stable housing arrangements for your children?" All my mom could do was sadly tell her, "No, I do not have a place for them to come to." This was a hard admission, since my mother didn't want them to know that we were homeless, because it meant my sister couldn't come home and I would be taken away too.

As my mother waited outside of the courtroom, our caseworker called around to different shelters for women with children. This was our last chance to be together if they could find a place for us. The caseworker slowly told my mother that there were no places for all of us. "We will have to take both the girls into the custody of the Department of Social Services; it is in their best interest. Don't worry, we'll find a safe place for each of them to be." With those words I was told to tell my mother goodbye. I could see how hard she wanted to cry and not let go of me. That is when I felt my heart drop. All I could do was follow the caseworker out of the courtroom and watch my mother cry as tears fell off of her face.

As I sat in the waiting room numbly waiting, I kept wondering as I would ask myself, "What did I get taken away from my mother for?" What did I do? Why was I the one who deserved this? What did I do wrong?" I felt as if I was being punished for something I didn't do. I felt as if I just didn't matter to anybody.

As I went from foster home to foster home, I became a hard child to deal with. I was so confused and angry all the time. I started having problems at school. I wasn't able to concentrate on my work. I became severely depressed. I hated myself. Other kids made fun of me, a foster child; my life felt like it was over. In foster care, everything I wanted to do needed to be approved by a caseworker. I wasn't able to be a normal child. I would be so depressed I would sit in my room and write poems that tried to tell others how I felt and what I wanted in my life. I felt like I was hiding in the dark until someone would listen to me and shine a light to guide me through. I never knew how hard it could be to stay in the system.

My behavior finally caused me to be placed in Diana's home, the last chance for children like me. I was with Diana and her family for over a year and it was the first time I felt heard. I felt seen. Finally, I was in the safe place they had promised me so long ago.

Free At Last
by Lise Anna

I was once a child so many years ago
My innocence was stolen from me
I would never be the same again
My mother didn't believe me
And too frightened to tell anyone else
I lived in fear and shame
My brain no longer thought like that of a child
My soul became an adult long before its time
When others thought of
what games they would play
I thought of what books that
I could become a part of
When others were playing with Barbie™ Dolls
I was soaring with eagles high in the sky
Riding wild horses through the untamed land
No one could catch me, I was too fast
In my mind I was free at last

Can the Cycle Be Broken?
by Lise Anna

Her brown curly hair and hazel eyes
She has a smile that melts my heart
With all my soul, I love her like no other
Her strong willed personality and stubborn attitude
Quick tempered and hard headed,
she doesn't like to listen
Nasty tantrums, loud screams, constant whining
Tempers flare, quick to lose control
Suddenly shaking,
aware of what almost happened
It came so close, barely able to stop
Feeling failure and deep shame
Unable to stop crying,
unable to stop wondering
Can the cycle be broken?

RESPECT
by Jenny

Respect him?
My mom pleaded with me.
But you have to give respect, to get respect.
My mom loves him so much,
and I suppose he loves her too.

Everyone tells me to accept him.
To look at him as a father.
But why should I? He doesn't act like one?
Why should I call him dad?

He makes her feel guilty.
Guilty for loving her own children.
He tells her how bad she has raised her kids.
Does a real dad say that?

He picks her up from work.
We know he is harping on her.
She walks in slamming the door.
She screams for us and it all begins.

The yelling, fighting and bickering.
It's best if I let it run its course.
She yells at us, because of him.
So, I ask you, "Does he deserve respect?"

Not Like TV
by Misty

To start off, I grew up in placement since I was three years old. I didn't have a very good home. This is one thing that made me have problems with other people. I always feel they are going to leave me, so I mess up and leave them first. Some people cared and stuck on, but most others just gave up because it was too hard.

Diana never gave up, even though I wasn't the easiest kid in her home. I used to think that I was worthless and that I wanted to die when I moved to Diana's. I felt I was alone and I made it difficult for her and her family. But now I see it could've been worked out. Maybe if I wasn't so argumentative, things wouldn't have gotten so hard. If I could turn back time, I would change everything. Maybe my past would have led to a different future.

Now I'm back in an institution where I started off in the beginning. I'm back in jail once again, only now I have nothing. The food is horrible. And, if I ever thought the girls were mean at Diana's house, it's nothing compared to here. Now, I'm back to feeling like I want to die and I've started cutting a lot, too.

I guess all I'm saying is to take a look at your situation before it's too late. Is it really as bad as you think? Only now do I see that Diana's home was one of the best places I have been. She made me want to keep living and I didn't cut myself for a long time.

My story is real, and to be honest, not all stories are going to be like you see on TV. But, when I get this out, I hope you guys out there find hope within this book. What doesn't kill you really does make you stronger. So, God Bless and sleep with the angels, everyone...

Pick Me Up
by an adult survivor

It's so loud
Everything is spinning
Mommy is crying
Daddy seems to be winning

Furniture is flying
Daddy is screaming
Mommy, fetal, sobbing
What is the meaning?

Pick me up
I can make things better
If I don't help Mommy
Daddy's fists will get her.

Why won't you pick me up?
I'm scared and worried
Like I wasn't even there
They fought and they scurried.

It must be me
If I could talk I'd say 'sorry'.
I won't do it again
Daddy stop hitting Mommy!

A toddler, so small
I'm frightened and helpless
He won't let her get up
He's delirious, ruthless

Why can't I walk, talk, run, hide?
Just a baby in my crib, how will I survive?
She's not even moving
Is she even alive?

It's getting even louder
Don't they hear their noise?
I have to maintain composure
I can't lose my poise.

I think it's over
He's gone, I don't see him
Pick me up Mommy
If you can get up again.

Thickness in the air
Battle residue.
Don't come back Daddy
There's only room for two.

There's Something In The Way
by Crystal

There's something in the way....
Something that's always here...
Calling to me....
In things I don't understand.....
All that I want, yet, somehow, already have....
Is it a fear of the pain of death?
Possibly fear in the joy of life....
Still, there is a longing to be free......
A premonition to leave this place....
Desert what is mine....
To leave you all with the hurt I had carried for so
long.....
How would it end, if I took it all away?
Another statistic perhaps....
Perhaps I don't care...
I'm lying here dead, but I am breathing.....
A withering rose that crumbles to the soft kiss of the
night air....
Why did you leave me here to survive?
I never asked for anything....
Wipe away the tears upon drenched sleeve....
Crying, as I drown in the rain.....
You forgot to teach me how to swim.....
Never enough....
Never anything at all....
It was always something....

I'm Home
by Crystal

Sitting in that cell, staring out the window and somehow thinking I had won. Everything I had done, all of my crimes and drugs and through all of the lies, I really believed that I had triumphed over everyone who had ever condemned me. I would not be broken down and I would be the last person on earth before I ever let them tell me that my tribulations in life were a result of my own behavior. My cellmate and I had spent most of our time there boasting about the things we had done and places we had been. I was content in my own misery and well on my path of self-destruction. The system had cast me aside at the age of 14, with the belief that there was no hope for my recovery. I was a threat to society, a social misfit, another number in the files of the system...

After serving a partial sentence, I was given two options – I could finish out my sentence or I could accept placement in a foster home for no less than one year. Being the "street-savvy" person that I was, I was not going to pass up the opportunity to get back out onto the streets that harbored my addictions; I took the placement. Obviously, my plan was to merely pull the wool over everyone's eyes and continue on my path the way I had for sometime.

Going into my first foster home, I already held reservations from the horror stories I had heard in the past. Add those reservations to my already pessimistic attitude and it was a disaster from the get-go... I walked into that house with a smug, snotty little attitude. I would get my point across real quick that I was in total control and they had better get it! I acted out in every way I could possibly think of, just hoping they might take me back to jail.

One day, not too long after, I got my wish, after a heated argument with my foster mom about how ridiculous her "rules" were becoming and how they were only being directed toward me. I told her that I would never make it here and to put me back in jail or find me another place to stay. She agreed that I needed to be in a different placement and that she would do just that, but I would have to go back to jail until another place opened up. Then she proceeded to tell me what a worthless waste of space I was and how I should have been aborted while there was still hope...

Depression can seem like life is a never-ending battle once you allow yourself to hit rock bottom. I allowed myself to sink even below rock bottom, everything and everyone was just a blur to me. I hated myself, but even more so, I hated everyone else for not seeing my battle and taking my hand. Back behind those cell walls, I was the perfect reflection of everything they had ever made me out to be. I tore down those who had anything positive to say about me; it was my goal to make everyone feel as alone and broken down as I did.

All of the girls in detention were just another form of me, all from broken homes and distraught lives filled with abuse of every kind. All of us were just struggling so hard to be seen by anyone, and it was no matter what that might take. We cried together, laughed together, and fought together – but most of all, we died together... Everyday in that place without notice, we each died a little bit more inside, lost a little more of who we were and who we once wanted to become.

Eventually, I was told that another placement had opened up and I would be the first kid ever to be placed in their home. I was hesitant to say that I would love to be anywhere other than the jail I had come to know as home. But, on the other hand, it was yet another opportunity to get back out into "my life," which was really only the sick delusion I forced myself into believing was real.

Walking in the door of the house, I greeted Diana and her family politely and thought to myself, "This will be a piece of cake." I stayed awake until the early morning hours talking and spilling my guts to her, just to get a head start on my empathy points. I had learned very early on that telling everyone all the details about what a horrible life I had endured seemed to do just that. It would often soften their heart ever so much, just enough that I could begin to bend it to suit my needs.

However, when I went to bed that morning, I had just a slightly different feeling than I had ever gotten before. Normally I would go through the motions and get the strong feeling that I was being listened to simply because it was a requirement to being on the state's payroll. This time was different somehow, Diana not only listened to what I was saying, but she had shared personal things about herself as well. In a way, I figured that this was a way of getting me to open up to what was really going on and try to get me to break down to one of the mushy crybabies that I had resented in my other placements. Then I thought she really had no reason for telling me all of that other than she wanted me to know that in some way she could relate.

I remember one day when she surprised us all with a shopping trip! She allowed us to pick out a ton of clothes and things that we wanted and needed to be enrolled in school within the days to follow. It was the first time in a long time that I had felt any sense of normalcy. I wanted to harbor this secret hatred for her so badly, but with every small thing she did to show us she cared, my hatred slipped farther and farther into the back of my mind. Walking through the mall that day was not a required field trip with the foster family; it was just a fun day out with the girls. That was the one thing I always remember respecting about Diana, she was always a parent when she needed to be, but at the same time, she knew when to just sit back and act like a friend. That day was not a day for structure and reflection on the reasons we were where we were. It was merely a day to see the things that could be, a life outside of our constant insanity.

Going to school is all it took to put me right back where I started, the feelings as well as the trouble. I was again defiant against any request that was made of me. I was getting right back into my old patterns and it felt good to be returning to the insanity that I knew as normal. Before long I had pushed it all too far, again...

I returned home one night to find Diana in tears and saying, "I didn't want for any of this to happen; I just can't handle your behavior anymore. I need for you to spend a few days at a respite home, while I regroup and come up with a better way of helping you."

I snapped back, "Why did you ever even bother if you were only going to give up on me just like everyone else?"

She smiled at me to try and hide the tears that were welling up in her eyes and said, "It's not for good, I just have to have some time to think, I promise."

I arrived at the respite house around dinner time that evening. They asked me to join them for dinner and I snidely declined the offer and asked if I could go to bed early. I remember lying awake that night in a complete daze about the whole day's events. Then, for no reason at all, I began to *genuinely* cry for the first time in almost a year! It was the longest, hardest night I had ever had, as I finally began to face all of the ugly truths about the way I was living out my life. I finally established that maybe people weren't leaving me because of who I was; maybe they were leaving because they couldn't handle seeing me *not* being the person I could be!

I wrote more poetry in those few days than I had been able to write for sometime, and my heart was finally beginning to lighten. I made up my mind that, if she would have me, I would return to Diana's home and appreciate a little more of what I had. I made a vow that I wanted to be that person everyone told me they saw in me, and that I was going to make a solid attempt to change starting right then!

I left the respite home within a few days, excited to tell about some of the things I had realized over the days passed. My stomach was in knots, as I had been told my real mom would be there to discuss options... Plus, I had no idea if Diana would even take me back into her home; I only hoped that she would see the sincerity of my apology...

Finally, I mustered up some courage and walked inside. I gave my real mom a hug and immediately started to weep to her of how I was sorry and that I loved her very much. She returned the sentiment and hugged me tighter than ever before. The look on her face was one I had longed for, a proud parent finding her lost daughter after many years of searching.

I turned to Diana and she was there already standing and waiting to embrace me. I hugged her and told her that I was sorry for putting her through this much anguish and that she never had to put herself in the middle of all my problems. I understood now that she did it only out of sole concern for us kids, that her love ran as deep as any real parent's love, and she had been there for us all more than a lot of real parents would endure to be.

We sat down and began setting up new rules of conduct. Needless to say, I liked the new feeling I had running through me and I knew this was the best place I could possibly be to continue that feeling, so I agreed to the guidelines. It was yet another long and emotionally draining day as we hashed out everything that was expected of me in the time to come, but I couldn't help but smile lying in bed that night because, for the first time in a long time, I felt like I was home.

Fists Of Fury
by Crystal

Fear is what holds you here
In the fists of his fury
Take a look at the terror of your heart
Remember your pain and speak of truth

Look into that child's eyes, into his future
Tell him your lies of what it may hold
His upbringing, no excuse for this hurt
It should have been one of teaching
Something to make him change those ways

Why must we live this way?
In this continuous hell
Tell me that baby doesn't know
He sees right through the fake smiles of a crying
mommy

Comfort him now
Say it'll be all right
In your heart you know the truth
It won't end here

Next time
A little bit harder
A little more apologetic
It's the last tear this time right?
Merely because you have none left for tomorrow

Can you really become immune?
To all his lies and kisses
An "I'm sorry" to stop your external crying
A punch to regain the internal pain

Now, look into your eyes
Can you see yourself anymore?
Are you content living through his hate?
Playing out the routine to cover it up

Tell your son why
Daddy hits Mommy
Your explanations won't help when his hate becomes
the same
When his pass down to be
Fists of Fury...

Shadows In The Night
by Lise Anna

Night is here once again
Fear overrides my sleep
It will keep me awake till dawn
When I can finally close my eyes

I welcome the darkness
It makes it easier to be unseen
I fear the echo of footsteps
It searches for where I might hide

When will it all end
This overwhelming fear of mine
I am exhausted and weary
I cannot go on

I know it is time to stop running
My weary soul must rest
It is time to face the shadows
That stalked me in the night

Love Divine
by Sheila

He paused before the Great White Throne.
A timid, trembling, weary child:
With lowered eyes he stood alone,
The Master saw, and gently smiled.

"You come alone- your parents Son.
Are they not in this great vast throng?"
"Master, I fear that there are none,
The child said low, "I don't belong."

He pointed to the multitude-
"Look child! You have a mother sure,
And father who in gratitude
Received the love of one so pure."

The childish voice came low and clear,
"They did not want me, Sir, to love."
He hung his head, "So I came here
To find the Father up above."

Then from the crowd a trembling hand
Outstretched, a humble, broken voice
Entreated, "Lord, you understand
I love him now. I will rejoice,

If but to clasp his curly head
Close to my heart." The young child turned,
"Is she the mother, Sir," he said,
"That the touch of my baby hands has spurned?"

And further back in trembling tone
A man's voice rose up pleadingly-
"Master, he's mine, my very own
His hands shall be all heaven to me!"

"These are your parents, child," His voice
Brought tears to wistful eyes of blue,
Timid the answer, "Sir, I heard-
But Master, I'd rather stay with you."

Then from the throne the Master stepped,
Upon His face, the Love Divine,
With curly head clasped to His breast
"I say unto you," He said, "he's Mine."

Dear Mother,

The decision to write in your book was not an easy one; however, your courage to finally let the world know your childhood has been the inspiration I needed to find the bravery within myself to share this small part of my past. After learning about how poorly society has reacted to your past struggles, I have realized that you are doing this out of love for not only me, but also every other child who is hurting inside. You are sharing your whole life story with the hope of improving someone else's. I want to help. As a child I had my self worth stripped away without anyone looking into my eyes to find my pain and I want people to finally see the effects that has had on me to this day. I am now an adult, who through a number of self-destructive ways, has been searching for my purpose.

I lived with my biological mother until I was twelve years old and began running away from home. My mom and step-father didn't know what to do, so they put me in a hospital. While in the hospital, I had to attend therapy sessions to help figure out what was wrong at home. At first, I was hesitant to talk because I was afraid of how the counselors would react after hearing what I had to tell them.

After a day at the ropes course, I had finally learned that I could trust again and I started to open up in therapy. I told the counselor that my step-father had sexually abused me from the age of five until the age of 10, until one day when he just stopped. They asked me a lot of embarrassing questions and as I answered each one I felt so ashamed. All I wanted was for my mom to come comfort me. That never happened though. Instead of providing comfort and support, she turned against me. She accused me of lying to break them up so I could have my way. My whole family believed her; I was the liar.

Because my mom took my step-father's side over mine, I was removed from my house and put in a foster home. Foster homes are the loneliest places in the world! Strangers come and take you from everything that is familiar, changing your whole life in a matter of minutes, and not once do they ask what you want or how you feel.

Social Services is a sad and lonely place to be. No one there truly sees you or understands your pain. All they worry about is where they are going to put you and how it will be paid for.

I ran from every foster home I was put in, so finally a judge ordered me to live in a group home. I thought foster homes were the loneliest places I'd find myelf, group homes are even lonelier, because now you are with a staff instead of a family and you are treated more like a problem than a child who is lost. I was on the run again, but of course you can only live on the streets for so long before people get tired of you, and unless you want to sleep on a bench and eat from the trash, you eventually turn yourself in, if you don't get caught first. I, being the girly girl that I am, usually turned myself in. I would rather be warm and alone than freezing on a bench and alone.

After running from the group homes so many times, the judge ordered me to live in a girl's locked down facility. I think you are all getting the point here; instead of anyone ever saying I love you, let me help you, let me try to understand and give you your life back, the system just kept punishing me and putting me more and more in a dark and isolated corner. Then one day a friend who had watched me grow up since I was seven said, "Let me love her. Let my family give her back her life." That friend is Diana Joy, the woman I now call my mother.

When I first got to my mom's house, it was great. It felt so good to be with a family I knew and trusted. That feeling of comfort didn't last long because I had already been ignored and alone for so long that I didn't know how to let her and my dad love me without being angry. I tried to push them away, but they never gave up on me.

Eventually, they realized I had to deal with my anger on my own, but they never stopped loving me or letting me know that I wasn't alone anymore. They saw my pain. They knew I was hurting, that I wasn't just a problem, but I was a child who was lost and needed help. I couldn't see that then because I felt safer being alone. I didn't want to be loved. I didn't feel I was worth it. I know how much my family loves me, and I know that what happened wasn't my fault, but even as an adult I struggle with knowing I am worth more than the streets.

I am in my early twenties now, and everyday I have to tell myself I can face the world. I am surrounded by my children who adore me and my friends and family who all support me, yet there is still a part of me that feels like I am living in a dark room and no one can hear me. I still feel like no one loves me, that I will never be enough for anyone, and I let people walk over me because I feel like I deserve it. I always think if I have this or that I won't feel lonely, so I get it but the emptiness is still there. So I think of something else that will make me feel better, but it never changes anything. Even now, as I sit here writing this, I think to myself, if I had a husband who loved me and my children, then I would be ok. But deep down I know that's not true. I would still be all alone inside.

I purposefully ruin my life every time it goes well because I don't know what to do when I'm not in chaos. I fall apart and my life is a mess. My family and my children suffer for it, and I eventually hit bottom. I always get back up again and fix everything, but it only lasts for a while. I have managed to keep my life together for 11 months now, and it is starting to fall apart again, but this time I realize what is happening. I am trying my hardest to keep it together. I remind myself twenty times a day that I deserve what I have and I am worth more than what I allow myself to be.

I hope you can take something from me, and the next time you see a child in trouble, don't turn away from them. Give them a hug.

Everyday we see children acting out, and we think to ourselves, "Look at that child. They are horrible." Reality is that child is just scared and hurt, and if you ignore them long enough they will go away and no one may ever see true joy in their eyes again. Please listen to the stories in this book and remember what it was like for you as a child. Some of you are thinking of all the fun times you had and your family vacations. Others of you are thinking of beatings that you got or nights when nightmares were your reality. Whoever you are, it is never too late to reach out to someone. I hope together lives will be changed because of my mom and all of the other brave people in this book.

Love,
Your Child Without A Birth Certificate

Conclusion

Thank you for walking through the lives of all the children within these pages and thank you for continuing to pray with us for our future and our children. If you are one who needs to be seen, or would like to help others be seen, please feel safe to connect with us through our website – www.unseenchild.com.

I speak of many verses in the Bible. But as I conclude this book, one will shine above all others!

"I pray that out of his glorious riches he may strengthen you with power through his Spirit in your inner being, so that Christ may dwell in your hearts through faith. And I pray that you, being rooted and established in love, may have power, together with all the saints, to grasp how wide and long and high and deep is the love of Christ, and to know this love that surpasses knowledge—that you may be filled to the measure of all the fullness of God. Now to him who is able to do immeasurably more than all we ask or imagine, according to his power that is at work within us, to him be glory in the church and in Christ Jesus throughout all generations, for ever and ever!

Amen. (Ephesians 3:16-21)"

Diana Joy's Unseen Friends

Peter: *a boy about 13*

Little Mother: *a young woman*

Crystal: *a girl about 5*

Sue & Dee: *twin girls about 3*

Ruby: *a girl in her early teens*

Midnight: *a girl in her teens*

Shadow: *a boy about 10*

Diane: *a girl who is always the same age as Diana*

Deanna: *a girl about 12*

Willie: *a boy about 5*

Diana was an unseen child. She was one of six unseen children in her family. This book tells of the unspeakable crimes perpetuated upon her and her siblings because no one saw them - and no one heard these children cry out.

Diana has taken her mission in life from these experiences, dedicating her life to helping the 'unseen children' of today. She has successfully raised her own children, raised adopted children and raised foster children. Now, she is focused on all the other unseen children and is willing to do even more for them, but she is only one person and there is an amazing amount of work to be done.

By writing her story, Diana is empowering society to recognize these children. She knows once you truly see them, you too will be inspired to help them to become seen by all, to get help, to heal and most importantly, to be sure they will be able to break the cycle of abuse.

Our Heartfelt Thanks Goes out to Our Sponsors

Felisha K. Scott of the Healing Club
HealingClub.com

1clickindustries.com

Susie McEntire Luchsinger
SusieLuchsinger.com

Mark Crowley & David Sandusky
Greenwood Village
Chamber of Commerce
GVChamber.com

& Your Brand Radio
YourBrandRadio.com

Woman Of
WomenOf.com

Colorado Business Women (DTC)
dtc-cbw.org

Recommended Resources

Heaven Help Me Raise These Children
by Janey L. DeMeo   ISBN: 2950946402
* Highly recommended by Diana Joy

Multiple Victimization of Children: Conceptual, Development, Research, and Treatment Issues
by Betty B. Rossman and Mindy S. Rosenberg
                    ISBN: 0789003619
* A chapter in this book is a case study of Diana Joy.

What Will Set You Free
by Cynthia James   ISBN: 0982083874
* A non-fiction / self help book intended to help adult survivors a violent childhoods.

Bobby's Story
by J. Richard Knapp   ISBN: 0977476170
* A fiction novel based on real events written by a school principal empowering teenagers to stand up for themselves.

I Have a Secret, Do I Keep It?
by EJ Thornton   **ISBN: 1932344667**
* A children's book for ages 3-8 teaching them when it safe to keep a secret and when it is not!

Angel On Board
by EJ Thornton   **ISBN: 1932344764**
* A fiction novel credited with being able to help the bereaved.

Felisha K. Scott of the The Healing Club
* The Healing Club is a place where victims and survivors of domestic violence can network, get support, and obtain helpful resources which will provide them with tools to move forward to a healthier and happier life.

"Where People Heal & Rebuild"

www.healingclub.com

Unseen Child Foundation

unseenchild.com

HOW YOU CAN HELP
REACH THE UNSEEN CHILDREN
OF THE WORLD!

I get so many requests asking, "Diana, how can I help you?" Well, here are some simple ways you can get involved...

I'm ready to go where others will not! I'm ready to speak for those who cannot! I want to help the unseen children who are hiding in the shadows of life!

Please help me get into the prisons, the rehabilitation centers, the shelters and safe houses, the schools, the libraries, the churches, and the neigborhoods where these hurting children can be found...

I've got the passion and I've got the message, I simply need financial support.

Costs include travel, lodging, meals, and MOST IMPORTANTLY - the funds to be able to print and distribute copies of *Looking through the Eyes of an Unseen Child* into the hands of everyone in need.

Some of those who need to read this book the most are unable to afford to purchase a copy of their own...

A portion of the profits from every book sold is donated to the Unseen Child Foundation to help keep this mission strong so that it can help the children.

A special thanks goes out to our website designer and sponsor, Eriq.

Order Form

Looking Through the Eyes of an Unseen Child

$19.^{95} + 2.^{50} (S&H)

online at: www.BooksToBelieveIn.com
www.UnseenChild.com

by phone: (303) 794-8888

by fax: (720) 863-2013

by mail:
send check payable to:

Books To Believe In, Inc.
17011 Lincoln Ave. #408
Parker, Colorado 80134

If it is temporarily sold out at your favorite bookstore,
have them order more of ISBN: 0-9824705-0-9

Name: _____
Address _____
_____
Phone: _____
E-mail: _____

Credit Card #: _____
Card Type: _____   Expiration Date: ____/____
Security Code: _____